PS3561.O455 T36 2013

Komunyakaa, Yusef

Testimony: a tribute to
Charlie Parker with new
and selected jazz poems

DATE DUE

DEMCO, INC. 38-2931

YUSEF
KOMUNYAKAA

Including the complete
Australian Broadcasting
Corporation audio
recording with music
by Sandy Evans

Commentaries
by Sandy Evans,
Sascha Feinstein,
Paul Grabowsky,
Christopher Williams,
and Miriam Zolin

Project Editor, Victoria Stahl

Wesleyan University Press | Middletown, Connecticut

Testimony

A TRIBUTE TO
CHARLIE PARKER

WITH NEW AND
SELECTED JAZZ POEMS

Wesleyan University Press
Middletown, CT 06459
www.wesleyan.edu/wespress

Wesleyan University Press is a member of the Green
Press Initiative. The paper used in this book meets
their minimum requirement for recycled paper.

Library of Congress Cataloging-in-Publication
data available upon request.

4   3   2   1

Original recording of *Testimony* (P) 2013
Australian Broadcasting Corporation.
RECORDING LICENSED COURTESY OF
AUSTRALIAN BROADCASTING CORPORATION.

ART WORKS.
arts.gov

This project is supported in part
by an award from the National
Endowment for the Arts

CONTENTS

Foreword, Sascha Feinstein   vii

PART ONE   Jazz Poems, Yusef Komunyakaa   1

Rhythm Method   3

Togetherness   5

Twilight Seduction   6

Woman, I Got the Blues   9

Jasmine   10

Gingkoes   12

Tenebrae   13

Cante Jondo   16

Changes; or, Reveries at a Window
   Overlooking a Country Road, with Two Women
   Talking Blues in the Kitchen   19

The Same Beat   22

To Beauty   24

Ignis Fatuus   26

Pepper   27

Satchmo, USA   29

Nightbird   32

Copacetic Mingus   33

Gerry's Jazz   34

Speed Ball   36

February in Sydney   37

The Plea   38

Elegy for Thelonious   40

Dolphy's Aviary   42

Gutbucket   43

Blue Light Lounge Sutra for the Performance
   Poets at Harold Park Hotel   44

The Story of a Coat   46

No-Good Blues   48

Ode to the Saxophone   54

Coda   55

PART TWO   *Testimony*, Yusef Komunyakaa and Sandy Evans   57

THE LIBRETTO

Yusef Komunyakaa's "Testimony" and the Humanity
     of Charlie Parker
     Sascha Feinstein   61

Survival Masks: An Interview with Yusef Komunyakaa
     Sascha Feinstein   69

Testimony
     Yusef Komunyakaa   79

THE MUSIC

Testimony, The Ties that Bind
     Miriam Zolin   95

French Flowers Blooming: The Music for *Testimony*
     Sandy Evans and Christopher Williams   105

Composer/Musical Director's Notes
     Sandy Evans   111

Testimony, Songs and Musicians
     Sandy Evans   115

Australian Art Orchestra Performances
     Paul Grabowsky   121

Contributors   125

Selected Bibliography   131

Selected Discography   133

Acknowledgments   137

Testimony, The Recording   139

FOREWORD

Sascha Feinstein

In 1997, the same year Yusef Komunyakaa completed "Testimony," his libretto for Charlie Parker, he flew to Chicago to perform live with a jazz sextet led by multi-reed instrumentalist John Tchicai and bassist Fred Hopkins. Released the following year on the CD *Love Notes from the Madhouse*, the session would go so well that Tchicai later gushed, "There might have been angels among us." The group opened with the poem "Ode to a Drum," the first few words a cappella, Komunyakaa's tone like rum-soaked chocolate: "Gazelle, I killed you / for your skin's exquisite / touch."

Incremental accompaniment—drums at first, then bass—allowed the group members to introduce themselves. But Komunyakaa's first words, just a grace note over two lines, also provide an introduction for the jazz poems collected here. The physicality of jazz—touching drum skins, plucking strings, pressing lips onto mouthpieces—matters a great deal to Komunyakaa, but to an even greater extent, so do the multiple implications of imagery. In this particular case, the slaughtered gazelle evokes so much complexity inherent to the instrument: sacrifice, beauty, sensuality, sound. Once touched, the nature of this skin becomes as elemental as its voice, in keeping with the heartbeat of this book's opening poem, "Rhythm Method": "*oh yes* / is a confirmation the skin / sings to hands."

Other jazz poems by Komunyakaa expand on this imagery of body and soul. Skin provides mystery, as seen in "No-Good Blues" ("this secret song from the soil / left hidden under my skin") and "Gerry's Jazz" ("each secret / is buried beneath the skin"). In "February in Sydney," a related allusion speaks to tragic realities of abuse: "A loneliness / lingers like a silver needle / under my black skin"—an image that prefigures the refrain in "Tenebrae" ("You try to beat loneliness / out of a drum"). In "Twilight Seduction," the reference evokes sexuality and touch: "The drum / can never be a woman, / even if her name's whispered / across skin." And such references and experiences are never exclusive; in these poems and most others, Komunyakaa has mastered the art of braiding emotional extremes.

That ability has been evident from the start of his prestigious career. Consider, for example, poems reprinted from his first full-length collection, *Copacetic*—the "senseless beauty" in "Elegy for Thelonious" (similar, of course, to Monk's tune "Ugly Beauty"), or the echo of "hard love" in "Copacetic Mingus." Any blues artist will tell you that the most significant details in sung lyrics—the time of day, a train whistle from the hills, the flight and sound of a mockingbird—inhabit the duality of the blues, which is to say, not one meaning or another but a fusion of opposites. Joy married to longing. Departure as a form of arrival. Independence a mirror image for isolation. To categorize emotions is to betray our humanity—and every poem by Komunyakaa denies such simplicity.

The title "February in Sydney," for example, conjures duality because of Australia's seasonal inversion to the Northern hemisphere—summer for winter—and given that geographical displacement, the speaker in that poem naturally turns to jazz expatriates, starting with Dexter Gordon and drifting to Bud Powell, Lester "Prez" Young, Ben Webster, and Coleman Hawkins. But that displacement also speaks to the alienation of African Americans in America, an "old anger" that rekindles a memory of racism. Although the speaker tries to separate emotional and moral extremes ("I try thinking something good, / letting the precious bad / settle to the salty bottom"), jazz itself emerges as a more truthful union of the two: sound as loneliness and triumph, art as pain and epiphany.

The very first section of "Testimony" also plays upon this theme. Speaking of Parker's formative years, Komunyakaa writes, "Maybe that's when he first / played laughter & crying / at the same time." By Section III, "Yardbird, he'd blow pain & glitter," and by VI, "Charlie could be two places at once." Again, Komunyakaa celebrates the emotional complexity of human experience by fusing opposites. Setting the poem to music, therefore, required equal expansiveness in thought and sound. In the past, Komunyakaa's poetry has been performed to many styles of music, from contemporary classical to southern blues, but no individual poem of his has created a greater challenge for a composer.

If I came to "Testimony" and the other poems in this book with the warmth of known memory, I listened to these recordings with the joy of surprise and the deep pleasure of new friendships. From the introductory dissection of Bird tunes to the final notes from a solo alto, the compositions performed here under the leadership of the multi-talented Sandy Evans nearly overwhelm the listener with their diversity and aesthetic vitality. Evans never parrots the sound of Charlie Parker, nor does she ever opt for easy, referential gestures; instead, her compositions speak to Parker's breadth as a musician, as well as Komunyakaa's poetic lines, and the effect has the weighty intensity of opera. Like the libretto itself, it capitalizes on the textures of different voices and rhythms while at the same time surging forward, never lagging.

I cannot overstate the difficulty of Evans' accomplishment, nor would I dare attempt to summarize her layered music. Tune to tune, passage to passage, we encounter tapestries of sound that play to and off one another. Call and response. Lush melody to atonality. Scripted composition to scat. Swing, bebop, church-like grooves, R & B, samba, even modern classical— the variety here both challenges and excites our ears. And forget what you think you know: No matter how familiar you may be with the infamous telegrams that Charlie Parker sent to his wife—quoted by Komunyakaa in Section X and performed as "Pree's Funeral Song"—when you hear the actor Michael Edward-Stevens embody the language, a part of you will break.

Such artistic and emotional surprises abound on these two recordings, and the achievement highlights an obvious counter truth: It's *easy* to wreck poetry with sound, and it's equally easy to deaden swing with stilted narratives. I braced myself, for example, for the performance of Section III ("Purple Dress") because the gorgeous imagery in those passages resists further ornamentation; with an uninspired melodic line or an insecure performer, beauty could wither. Those lines of poetry in particular already embrace the power of synesthesia; they proclaim and demonstrate how

Bird "could blow / insinuation." But hearing his known lines *sung*—and sung with such sensitivity by Kristen Cornwell—transforms the stanzas into something entirely fresh and memorable, an experience in keeping with the essence of jazz.

The brief quote above reminds me of Komunyakaa's poem titled "Insinuations," which concludes by referencing another brilliant alto saxophonist: "We said we didn't know why / we loved walking in the rain / 'til everything disappeared, / but knew why Eric Dolphy / pried the lids off skulls." Indeed, many of his poems that don't appear in this book acknowledge blues and jazz musicians, if only in passing, and no reference is more intriguing than his allusion in the justly famous "My Father's Love Letters," where the child of a beaten mother "sometimes wanted / To slip in a reminder, how Mary Lou / Williams' 'Polka Dots & Moonbeams' / Never made the swelling go down." (As far as I know, Williams never waxed that tune, and yet the created music—that is, the artistry of Williams as recreated by Komunyakaa—seems exactly right for that poem.) Nor do mere allusions, of course, represent the full influence of jazz; if we're to discuss the musicality of Komunyakaa's verse, then references must give way to his own achievements in rhythm and harmony, spotlit by the ecstatic finale of "Blue Light Lounge Sutra":

> the need gotta be basic
> animal need to see
> & know the terror
> we are made of honey
> cause if you wanna dance
> this boogie be ready
> to let the devil use your head
> for a drum.

The poem "Twilight Seduction" informs us of the "wishbone" connecting Komunyakaa to Duke Ellington—a common birth date—yet they share so much more. Just as Ellington's creative drive seemed inexhaustible, so does Komunyakaa's expansive and expanding outpouring of literature speak to his urgent devotion to the craft. Ellington created many works that were "beyond category," and the same can be said of Komunyakaa. (His piece "Buddy's Monologue," for example, appears in *The Jazz Fiction Anthology*, but one could argue that it's a lengthy prose poem or, even more forcefully, that it's a vignette meant for the stage. In this collection, consider the innumerable ways of experiencing his poem "Changes; or, Reveries at a Window Overlooking a Country Road, with Two Women Talking Blues in the Kitchen.") No serious historical discussion about jazz can avoid the artistry of Duke Ellington, or Charlie Parker for that matter, and no serious discussion about the poetry of our time can ignore the artistry of Yusef Komunyakaa. As made obvious by these marvelous jazz poems—a captivating cross-section that bisects his poetry through just one of so many possible vectors—his cultural contributions are indispensable.

PART ONE

Jazz Poems

YUSEF

KOMUNYAKAA

If you were sealed inside a box
within a box deep in a forest,
with no birdsongs, no crickets
rubbing legs together, no leaves
letting go of mottled branches,
you'd still hear the rhythm
of your heart. A red tide
of beached fish oscillates in sand,
copulating beneath a full moon,
& we can call this the first
rhythm because sex is what
nudged the tongue awake
& taught the hand to hit
drums & embrace reed flutes
before they were worked
from wood & myth. Up
& down, in & out, the piston
drives a dream home. Water
drips 'til it sculpts a cup
into a slab of stone.
At first, no bigger
than a thimble, it holds
joy, but grows to measure
the rhythm of loneliness
that melts sugar in tea.
There's a season for snakes
to shed rainbows on the grass,
for locust to chant out of the dunghill.
Oh yes, oh yes, oh yes, oh yes
is a confirmation the skin
sings to hands. The Mantra
of spring rain opens the rose

& spider lily into shadow,
& someone plays the bones
'til they rise & live
again. We know the whole weight
depends on small silences
we fit ourselves into.
High heels at daybreak
is the saddest refrain.
If you can see blues
in the ocean, light & dark,
can feel worms ease through
a subterranean path
beneath each footstep,
Baby, you got rhythm.

TOGETHERNESS

Someone says Tristan
& Isolde, the shared cup
& broken vows binding them,
& someone else says Romeo
& Juliet, a lyre & Jew's harp
sighing a forbidden oath,
but I say a midnight horn
& a voice with a moody angel
inside, the two married rib
to rib. Of course, I am
thinking of those Tuesdays
or Thursdays at Billy Berg's
in L.A. when Lana Turner would say,
Please sing 'Strange Fruit'
for me, & then her dancing
nightlong with Mel Tormé,
as if she knew what it took
to make brass & flesh say *yes*
beneath the clandestine stars
& a spinning that is so fast
we can't feel the planet moving.
Is this why some of us fall
in & out of love? Did Lady Day
& Prez ever hold each other
& plead to those notorious gods?
I don't know. But I do know
even if a horn & voice plumb
the unknown, what remains unsaid
coalesces around an old blues
& begs with a hawk's yellow eyes.

TWILIGHT SEDUCTION

Because Duke's voice
    was smooth as new silk
        edged with Victorian lace, smooth

as Madame Zajj nude
    beneath her mink coat,
        I can't help but run

my hands over you at dusk.
    Hip to collarbone, right ear
        lobe to the sublime. Simply

because Jimmy Blanton
    died at twenty-three
        & his hands on the bass

still make me ashamed
    to hold you like an upright
        & a cross worked into one

embrace. Fingers pulse
    at a gold zipper, before
        the brain dances the body

into a field of poppies.
    Duke knew how to listen
        to colors, for each sigh shaped

out of sweat & blame,
    knew a Harlem airshaft
        could recall the whole

night in an echo: prayers,
    dogs barking, curses & blessings.
        Plunger mute tempered

by need & plea. He'd search
    for a flaw, a small scar,
        some mark of perfect

difference for his canvas.
    I hold your red shoes,
        one in each hand to balance

the sky, because Duke
    loved Toulouse-Lautrec's
        nightlife. Faces of women

woven into chords scribbled
    on hotel stationery—blues,
        but never that unlucky

green. April 29th
    is also my birthday,
        the suspicious wishbone

snapped between us,
    & I think I know why
        a pretty woman always

lingered *at the bass
    clef end of the piano.*
        Tricky Sam coaxed

an accented wa-wa
    from his trombone, coupled
        with Cootie & Bubber,

& Duke said, *Rufus,*
   give me some ching-chang
     & sticks on the wood.

I tell myself the drum
   can never be a woman,
     even if her name's whispered

across skin. Because
   nights at the Cotton Club
     shook on the bone,

because Paul Whiteman
   sat waiting for a riff
     he could walk away with

as feathers twirled
   among palm trees, because
     Duke created something good

& strong out of thirty pieces
   of silver like a spotlight
     on conked hair,

because so much flesh
   is left in each song,
     because women touch

themselves to know
   where music comes from,
     my fingers trace

your lips to open up
   the sky & let in
     the night.

WOMAN,
I GOT THE BLUES

I'm sporting a floppy existential sky-blue hat
when we meet in the Museum of Modern Art.

Later, we hold each other
with a gentleness that would break open
ripe fruit. Then we slow-drag
to Little Willie John, we bebop
to Bird LPs, bloodfunk, lungs paraphrased
'til we break each other's fall.
For us there's no reason the scorpion
has to become our faith healer.

Sweet Mercy, I worship
the curvature of your ass.
I build an altar in my head.
I kiss your breasts & forget my name.

Woman, I got the blues.
Our shadows on floral wallpaper
struggle with cold-blooded mythologies.
But there's a stillness in us
like the tip of a magenta mountain.

You're half-naked on the living-room floor
when the moon falls through the window
on you.

Your breath's a dewy flower stalk
leaning into sweaty air.

JASMINE

I sit beside two women, kitty-corner
to the stage, as Elvin's sticks blur
the club into a blue fantasia.
I thought my body had forgotten the Deep
South, how I'd cross the street
if a woman like these two walked
towards me, as if a cat traversed
my path beneath the evening star.
Which one is wearing jasmine?
If my grandmothers saw me now
they'd say, Boy, the devil never sleeps.
My mind is lost among November
cotton flowers, a soft rain on my face
as Richard Davis plucks the fat notes
of chance on his upright
leaning into the future.
The blonde, the brunette—
which one is scented with jasmine?
I can hear Duke in the right hand
& Basie in the left
as the young piano player
nudges us into the past.
The trumpet's almost kissed
by enough pain. Give him a few more years,
a few more ghosts to embrace—Clifford's
shadow on the edge of the stage.
The sign says, *No Talking*.
Elvin's guardian angel lingers
at the top of the stairs,
counting each drop of sweat
paid in tribute. The blonde
has her eyes closed, & the brunette

is looking at me. Our bodies
sway to each riff, the jasmine
rising from a valley somewhere
in Egypt, a white moon
opening countless false mouths
of laughter. The midnight
gatherers are boys & girls
with the headlights of trucks
aimed at their backs, because
their small hands refuse to wound
the knowing scent hidden in each bloom.

GINGKOES

When I retrace our footsteps
to Bloomington I recall talking jazz,
the half-forgotten South
in our mouths, the reptilian
brain swollen with manly regrets
left behind, thumbing volumes
inscribed to the dead in used
bookstores, & then rounding
griffins carved into limestone.
The gingkoes dropped fruit
at our feet & an old woman
scooped the smelly medicine
into a red plastic bucket,
laughing. We walked across
the green reciting Hayden,
& I still believe those hours
we could see through stone.
I don't remember the girls
in summer dresses strolling
out of the movie on Kirkwood,
but in the Runcible Spoon
sniffing the air, Cat Stevens
on a speaker, we tried to buy
back our souls with reveries
& coffee, the scent of bathos
on our scuffed shoes.

—for Christopher Gilbert

TENEBRAE

May your spirit sleep in peace
One grain of corn can fill the silo.
—the Samba of Tanzania

You try to beat loneliness
out of a drum,
but cries only spring
from your mouth.
Synapse & memory—
the day quivers like dancers
with bells on their feet,
weaving a path of songs
to bring you back,
to heal our future
with the old voices
we breathe. Sometimes
our hands hang like weights
anchoring us inside
ourselves. You can go
to Africa on a note
transfigured into a tribe
of silhouettes in a field
of reeds, & circling the Cape
of Good Hope you find
yourself in Paris
backing The Hot Five.

You try to beat loneliness
out of a drum.
As you ascend
the crescendo,
please help us touch what remains
most human. Your absence
brings us one step closer
to the whole cloth
& full measure.
We're under the orange trees again, as you work life
back into the double-headed
drumskin with a spasm
of fingertips
'til a chant leaps
into the dreamer's mouth.

You try to beat loneliness
out of a drum, always
coming back to opera & baseball.
A constellation of blood-tuned
notes shake against the night
forest bowed to the ground
by snow & ice. Yes,
this kind of solitude
can lift you up
between two thieves.

You can do a drum roll
that rattles slavechains
on the sea floor.
What wrong makes you
loop that silent knot
& step up on the gallows-
chair? What reminds you of the wounded paradise
we stumbled out of?

You try to beat loneliness
out of a drum,
searching for a note
of kindness here at the edge
of this grab-wheel,
with little or no dragline
beyond the flowering trees
where only ghosts live—
no grip to clutch the truth
under a façade of skylarks.

       —in memory of Richard Johnson

CANTE JONDO

Yes, I say, I know
    what you mean.
        Then we're off.

Improvising on what
    ifs: can you imagine
        Langston & Lorca

hypnotized at a window
    in Nella Larsen's
        apartment, pointing at

bridges & searchlights
    in a summer sky, can you
        see them? Their breath

clouds the windowpanes
    one puffed cloud
        indistinguishable from another.

They click their glasses
    of Jamaican rum. To your
        great King, says Lorca.

Prisoner in a janitor's suit,
    adds Langston. Their laughter
        ferries them to a sidestreet

in the Alhambra,
    & at that moment
        they see old Chorrojumo,

King of the Gypsies
     clapping his hands
          & stamping his feet

along with a woman dancing
     a rhumba to a tom-tom's
          rhythm. Is this Florence

Mills, or another face
     from the Cotton Club
          almost too handsome

to look at? To keep
     a dream of Andulusian
          cante jondo alive,

they agree to meet
     at Small's Paradise
          the next night,

where the bells of trumpets
     breathe honeysuckle & reefer,
          where women & men make love

to the air. You can see
     them now, reclining
          into the Jazz

Age. You can hear Lorca
     saying he cured his fear
          of falling from the SS Olympic

on the road to Alfacar.
    But the word sex doesn't
        flower in that heat wave

of 1929, only one man touching
    the other's sleeve, & hands
        swaying to "Beale Street Blues."

CHANGES; OR, REVERIES AT A WINDOW OVERLOOKING A COUNTRY ROAD, WITH TWO WOMEN TALKING BLUES IN THE KITCHEN

Joe, Gus, Sham...
Even George Edward
Done gone. Done
Gone to Jesus, honey.
Doncha mean the devil,
Mary? Those Johnson boys
Were only sweet talkers
& long, tall bootleggers.
Child, now you can count
The men we usedta know
On one hand. They done
Dropped like mayflies—
Cancer, heart trouble,
Blood pressure, sugar,
You name it, Eva Mae.
Amen. Tell the truth,
Girl. I don't know.
Maybe the world's heavy
On their shoulders. Maybe
Too much bed hopping
& skirt chasing
Caught up with them
God don't like ugly.
Look at my grandson
In there, just dragged in
From God only knows where.
He high tails it home
Inbetween women trouble.
He's nice as a new piece
Of silk. It's a wonder

Heat lighting jumpstarts the slow
afternoon & a syncopated rainfall
peppers the tin roof like Philly Joe
Jones' brushes reaching for a dusky
backbeat across the high hat. Rhythm
like cells multiplying... language &
notes made flesh. Accents & stresses,
almost sexual. Pleasure's knot; to wrestle
the mind down to unrelenting white space,
to fill each room with spring's contagious
changes. Words & music. "Ruby, My Dear"
turned down on the cassette payer,
pulsates underneath rustic voices
waltzing out the kitchen—my grandmama
& an old friend of hers from childhood
talking B-flat blues. Time & space,
painful notes, the whole thing wrung
out of silence. Changes. Caesuras.
Nina Simone's down-home cry echoes
theirs—Mister Backlash, Mister Backlash—
as a southern breeze herds wild, blood-
red roses along the barbed-wire fence.
There's something in this house, maybe
those two voices & Satchmo's gold horn,
refracting time & making the Harlem
Renaissance live inside my head.
I can hear Hughes like a river
of fingers over Willie 'The Lion" Smith's
piano, & some naked spiritual releases
a shadow in a reverie of robes & crosses.

Women don't stick to him
Like white on rice.
It's a fast world
Out there, honey
They go all kinda ways.
Just buried John Henry
With that old guitar
Cradled in his arms.
Over on Fourth Street
Singing 'bout hell hounds
When he dropped dead.
Your heard 'bout Jack,
Right? He just tilted over
In prayer meeting.
The good & the bad go
Into the same song.
How's Hattie? She
Still uppity & half
Trying to be white?
The man went off to war
& got one of his legs
Shot off & she wanted
To divorce him for that.
Crazy as a bessy bug.
Jack wasn't cold
In his grave before
She gone up & gave all
The insurance money
To some young pigeon
Who never hit a lick
At work in his life.
He cleaned her out & left
With Donna Faye's girl.
Honey, hush. You don't
Say. Her sister,
Charlene, was silly

Oriflamme & Judgment Day . . . undulant waves
bring in cries from Sharpeville & Soweto,
dragging up moans from shark-infested
seas as a blood moon rises. A shock
of sunlight breaks the mood & I hear
my father's voice growing young again,
as he says, "The devil's beating
his wife": One side of the road's rainy
& the other side's sunny. Imagination—
driftwood from a spring flood, stockpiled
by Furies. Changes. Pinetop's boogiewoogie
keys stack against each other like syllables
in tongue-tripped elegies for Lady Day
& Duke. Don't try to make any sense
out of this; just let it take you
like Prez's tenor & keep you human.
Voices of school girls rush & surge
through the windows, returning
with the late March wind; the same need
pushing my pen across the page.
Their dresses lyrical against the day's
sharp edges. Dark harmonies. Bright
as lamentations behind a spasm band
from New Orleans. A throng of boys
are throwing at a bloodhound barking
near a blaze of witch hazel at the corner
of the fence. Mister Backlash.
I close my eyes & feel castanetted
fingers on the spine, slow as Monk's
"Misterioso"; a man can hurt for years
before words flow into a pattern
so woman-smooth, soft as a pine-scented
breeze off the river Lethe. Satori-blue
changes. Syntax. Each naked string
tied to eternity—the backbone

Too. Jump into bed
With anything that wore
Pants. White, black,
Chinese, crazy, or old.
Some woman in Chicago
Hooked a blade into her.
Remember? Now don't say
You done forgot Charlene.
Her face a little blurred
But she coming back now.
Loud & clear. With those
Real big, sad, gray eyes.
A natural-born hell raiser,
& lose as persimmon pie.
You said it, honey.
Miss High Yellow.
I heard she's the reason
Frank shot down Otis Lee
Like a dog in The Blue
Moon. She was a blood-
Sucker. I hate to say this,
But she had Arthur
On a short leash too.
Your Arthur, Mary.
She was only a girl
When Arthur closed his eyes.
Thirteen at most.
She was doing what women do
Even then. I saw them
With my own two eyes,
& promised God Almighty
I wouldn't mention it.
But it don't hurt
To mention it now, not
After all these years.

strung like a bass. Magnolia
blossoms fall in the thick tremble
of Mingus's "Love Chant"; extended bars
natural as birds in trees & on power lines
singing between the cuts—Yardbird
in the soul & soil. Boplicity
takes me to Django's gypsy guitar
& Dunbar's "broken tongue," beyond
god-headed jive of the apocalypse,
& back to the old sorrow songs
where boisterous flowers still nod on their
half-broken stems. The deep rosewood
of the piano says, "Holler
if it feels good." Perfect tension.
The mainspring of notes & extended
possibility—what falls on either side
of a word—the beat between & underneath.
Organic, cellular space. Each riff & word
a part of the whole. A groove. New changes
created. "In the Land of Obladee"
burns out the bell with flatted fifths,
a matrix of blood & language
improvised on a bebop heart
that could stop any moment
on a dime, before going back
to Hughes at the Five Spot.
Twelve bars. Coltrane leafs through
the voluminous air for some note
to save us from ourselves.
The limbo & bridge of a solo . . .
trying to get beyond the tragedy
of always knowing what the right hand
will do . . . ready to let life play me
like Candido's drum.

THE SAME BEAT

I don't want the same beat.
I don't want the same beat.
I don't want the same beat
used for copping a plea
as well as for making love
& talking with the gods.

I don't want the same beat
like a windshield wiper
swishing back & forth
to the rhythm of stolen pain
& counterfeit pleasure.

I don't want the same beat
when I can listen to early
Miles, Prez, Yardbird, Sonny
Stitt, Monk, Lady Day, Trane,
or the Count of Red Bank.

I don't want the same beat
as I gaze out at the Grand Canyon
or up at the Dogstar
in a tenement window
or at an eagle who owns the air.

I don't want the same beat
as the buffoon on the turntable
selling his secondhand soul
to the organ-grinder's monkey.

I don't want the same beat
like a pitiful needle
stuck in a hyperbolic groove
at the end of The Causeway.

I don't want the same beat
as only background
for the skullduggery
of Iceberg Slim on a bullhorn.

I don't want the same beat
as the false witness,
because I know any man
with that much gold in his mouth
has already been bought & sold.

I don't want the
              same beat.
                                        I don't want the
same beat.
            I don't want the
              same beat.
I don't want the
              same beat.

TO BEAUTY

Just painting things black will get you nowhere.
—Otto Dix

The jazz drummer's
    midnight skin
        balances the whole

room, the American
    flag dangling from his breast
        pocket. An album

cover. "Everything
    I have ever seen is
        beautiful." A decade

before a caricaturist
    draws a Star of David
        for a saxophonist's lapel

on the poster of "Jonny
    spielt auf," his brush
        played every note & shade

of incarnadine darkness.
    Here's his self-portrait
        with telephone, as if

clutching a mike
    like Frank Sinatra—
        posed as an underworld

character, or poised
    for a dance step.
        Shimmy & Charleston.

Perfumed & cocksure,
    you'd never know
        he sat for hours

darning his trousers
    with a silver needle,
        stitching night shadows

to facade. The rosy lady's
    orange hair & corsage
        alight the dancefloor,

all their faces stopped
    with tempera & time.
        The drummer's shirt

the same hue & texture
    as a woman's dress,
        balanced on the edge

of some anticipated
    embrace. The yellow
        feathers of a rare bird

quiver in a dancer's hat,
    past the drum skin tattooed
        with an Indian chief.

IGNIS FATUUS

    Something or someone. A feeling
among a swish of reeds. A swampy
glow haloes the Spanish moss,
& there's a swaying at the edge
like a child's memory of abuse
growing flesh, living on what
a screech owl recalls. Nothing
but a presence that fills up
the mind, a replenished body
singing its way into doubletalk.
In the city, "Will o' the Wisp"
floats out of Miles' trumpet,
leaning ghosts against nighttime's
backdrop of neon. A foolish fire
can also start this way: before
you slide the key into the lock
& half-turn the knob, you know
someone has snuck into your life.
A high window, a corner of sky
spies on upturned drawers of underwear
& unanswered letters, on a tin box
of luminous buttons & subway tokens,
on books, magazines, & clothes
flung to the studio's floor,
his sweat lingering in the air.
Years ago, you followed someone
here, in love with breath
kissing the nape of your neck,
back when it was easy to be
at least two places at once.

PEPPER

If you were alive, Art
    Pepper, I'd collar you
  as you stepped off the

bandstand. Last notes
    of "Softly as in a Morning
  Sunrise" fall between us,

a hint of Africa
    still inside your alto.
  Someone wants to blame

your tongue on drugs: *If I*
    found out some white broad
  was married to a black guy

I'd rave at her in games
    & call her tramp, slut,
  whore. Did you steal

the Phoenix's ashes
    listening to Bird?
  I'm angry for loving

your horn these years,
    wooed by the monkey
  riding you in L.A.

as if changes in "Mambo
    De La Pinta" could be
  rounded off to less

than zero. Words
   you tried to take back
  left blood on the reed.

SATCHMO, USA

Dear Mr. Satchmo,
    I'm on the other side
        with "Tiger Rag" & "Way Down

Yonder in New Orleans"
    on the turntable, a heart
        drawn on the soles of my feet.

Here, in the inner sanctum,
    I see you toting buckets of coal
        to Storyville's red-light houses.

You are a small figure
    raising a pistol to fire
        at God in the night sky,

but when I turn to look
    out at the evening star
        your face is mine. You

are holding a bugle
    in your first cutting contest
        with fate. From back o'

town to the sphinx
    & Buckingham Palace,
        to the Cotton Club

& soccer fields in Africa, under
    spotlights with Ella & Billie
        one hundred nighttimes sweated up

from Congo Square. Listening
    to your notes across the river,
        the sea across miles of salt

trees, I hear a birth
    holler pushing through brass
        at the Lincoln Gardens

in '22 with Papa Joe,
    the Hot Five,
        the Hot Seven . . .

the sun on your horn
    makes me think this note
        can find you, Satchmo.

The Singing Brakeman
    beckoned you to Culver City
        to cut your deep light

into wax & Miss Lil
    followed trying to sew up
        a ragged seam. When you blow

I feel like you're talking
    to me, talking about Mayann
        & Mama Lucy as if

they're the same person—
    Lucille dancing on the edge
        of the stage—a loved one

selling fish in the Third Ward.
    In a corner of the naked
        eye, your smile isn't

a smile: confessions & curses
       drip from your trumpet,
              & notes about the FBI

dogging your footsteps
       since '48 float like ghosts
              of reefer smoke in an alley.

Ike wanted you to change
       your words about Little Rock
              as you wove hex signs

into "Indiana" & "Sleepy
       Down South." By the time
              that bomb in Memphis

settled into your mind,
       you were already back
              in Corona blowing triplets

for three or four boys
       sitting on your front steps.
              If you & your drummer

couldn't play on the same stage,
       New Orleans was only a bronze statue
              in a park. Satchmo, I believe

in your horn, how it takes us
       to a woman standing in a cane field
              circled with peacocks.

NIGHTBIRD

If she didn't sing the day
here, a votive sky
wouldn't be at the foot
of the trees. We're in
Rome at Teatro Sistina
on Ella's 40th birthday,
& she's in a cutting contest
with all the one-night stands.
"St. Louis Blues" pushes through
flesh 'til Chick Webb's here
beside her. A shadow
edges away from an eye,
& the clear bell of each note
echoes breath blown across
some mouth-hole of wood
& pumice. So many fingers
on the keys. She knows
not to ride the drums
too close, following the bass
down all the black alleys
of a subterranean heart.
The bird outside my window
mimics her, working songbooks
of Porter & Berlin into confetti
& grace notes. Some tangled laugh
& cry, human & sparrow,
scat through honey locust
leaves, wounded by thorns.

COPACETIC MINGUS

Mingus One, Two and Three.
Which is the image you want the world to see?
—Charles Mingus, *Beneath the Underdog*

Heartstring. Blessed wood
& every moment the thing's made of:
ball of fatback
licked by fingers of fire.
Hard love, it's hard love.
Running big hands down
the upright's wide hips,
rocking his moon-eyed mistress
with gold in her teeth.
Art & life bleed
into each other
as he works the bow.
But tonight we're both a long ways
from the Mile High City,
1973. Here in New Orleans
years below sea level,
I listen to *Pithecanthropus*
Erectus: Up & down, under
& over, every which way—
thump, thump, dada—ah, yes.
Wood heavy with tenderness,
Mingus fingers the loom
gone on Segovia,
dogging the raw strings
unwaxed with rosin.
Hyperbolic bass line. Oh, no!
Hard love, it's hard love.

GERRY'S JAZZ

At fourteen you crawl through a hole
in the wall where they slip sly grog
into Ollie Ward's Maxine Cabaret,
& listen to a band play for gangsters.
You're on your way to Tom Ugly's
& El Rocco, & the guns on tables

can't stop you. Something
takes back part of childhood pain,
riding out long hours behind the trap
as the sonorous high hat
clicks a fraction between the cracks,
& then you're off on a trip:

Gene Krupa's "Wire Brush Stomp"
rains over the kit & sizzles like a tin roof
after you hired a blacksmith
to hammer a cymbal into shape.
You rap sticks against it & sound travels
through everyone like rings of water.

Cocky & skillful, you go
into a groove & dance the true pivot,
playing for jitterbug
contests at Katoomba & the Trocadero.
Going deeper into each song,
you rattle keys like Houdini locked in a trunk,

bending within a black echo.
The difference
between the difference
is the difference, you holler
to a full moon hanging over
the steel mills of Wollongong.

Like an unknown voice rising
out of flesh, each secret
is buried beneath the skin,
& you feel they try to pick
your brain for them, to find
the rhythm of your heart,

as you swear the beat is stolen from the sea.
With empty flagons beside you at Fisherman's Bay,
you pat *Out of the Afternoon* upon your leg,
knowing you'll ride hope
'til it's nothing but a shiny bone
under heavy light.

SPEED BALL

Didn't Chet Baker know
They made each great white hope
Jump hoops of fire on the edge
Of midnight gigs that never happened?

Miles hipped him at The Lighthouse
About horse, said not to feel guilty
About *Down Beat* in '53. Chet stole
Gasoline to sniff, doctored with Beiderbecke's

Chicago style. But it wasn't long
Before he was a toothless lion
Gazing up at his face like a stranger's
Caught by tinted lens & brass. Steel–

Blue stare from Oklahoma whispering for
"A kind of high that scares everyone
To death." Maybe a bop angel, Slim
Greer, pulled him from that hotel window.

Dexter Gordon's tenor sax
plays "April in Paris"
inside my head all the way back
on the bus from Double Bay.
Round Midnight, the '50s,
cool cobblestone streets
resound footsteps of Bebop
musicians with whiskey-laced voices
from a boundless dream in French.
Bud, Prez, Webster, & The Hawk,
their names run together riffs.
Painful gods jive talk through
bloodstained reeds & shiny brass
where music is an anesthetic.
Unreadable faces float
like torn pages across the windshield.
An old anger drips into my throat,
& I try thinking something good,
letting the precious bad
settle to the salty bottom.
Another scene keeps repeating itself:
I emerge from the dark theatre,
passing a woman who grabs her red purse
& hugs it to her like a heart attack.
Tremolo. Dexter comes back to rest
behind my eyelids. A loneliness
lingers like a silver needle
under my black skin,
as I try to feel how it is
to scream for help through a horn.

THE PLEA

Round about midnight
   the clock's ugly stare
hangs in mental repose
   & its antimagnetic second hand
measures a man's descent.
   Bop, bop, bebop, rebop.
The bottom falls out
   of each dream—
the silver spike is
   in my hands & I'm on the floor.
The Alice in Malice
   does a little soft shoe
on my troubled heart.
   Hot & heavy,
cool & cosmic honeydripper
   fingers play the missing notes
inbetween life & death
   round midnight.
Bop, bop, bebop, rebop.
   Lost lovers in my empty doorway
groove to a sweet pain
   in the bruise-colored neon
where my soul weaves
   itself into *terra incognita*,
into the blue & green
   sounds of Botany Bay
reflected like rozellas
   through the big, black
slow dance of waves grinding against the shore.
   Bop, bop, bebop, rebop.

Thelonious & bright as that
    golden plea of gospel
under everything
    Monk wrung from the keys.
Round about midnight
    despair returns each minute
like a drop of moonshine
    elongating into rapture
moaned through Bird's mouthpiece
    in a soundproof room
where trust & love
    is white dust on the dark
furniture. Time is nothing
    but an endless bridge.
All those who thought
    they could use my body
for nowhere's roadmap
    I see their blank faces
float up from a whirlpool
    as the turntable spins.
Bop, bob, bebop, rebop.
    Each undying note
resounds in my head;
    there's a cry in every pocket
& low swell of unhappy
    lust I've suffered,
& round about midnight the odor of sex
    & salvation quivers in each song
the wooden hammers
    strike from wire strings
like anger stolen back
    from the soil.

Damn the snow.
Its senseless beauty
pours a hard light
through the hemlock.
Thelonious is dead. Winter
drifts in the hourglass;
notes pour from the brain cup.
Damn the alley cat
wailing a muted dirge
off Lenox Ave.
Thelonious is dead.
Tonight's a lazy rhapsody of shadows
swaying to blue vertigo
& metaphysical funk.
Black trees in the wind.
"Crepuscule with Nellie"
plays inside the bowed head.
Dig the Man Ray of piano!
O Satisfaction,
hot fingers blur
on those white rib keys.
"Coming on the Hudson."
"Monk's Dream."
The ghost of bebop
from 52nd Street,
footprints in the snow.
Damn February.
Let's go to Minton's
& play "modern malice"

'til daybreak. Lord,
there's Thelonious
wearing that old funky hat
pulled down over his eyes.

DOLPHY'S AVIARY

We watched Baghdad's skyline
ignite, arms & legs entwined
as white phosphorus washed over
our bedroom, the sounds of war
turned down to a sigh. It was one
of those nights we couldn't let go
of each other, a midwestern storm
pressing panes 'til they trembled
in their sashes. Eric Dolphy
scored the firmament splitting
to bedrock, as the wind spoke
tongues we tried to answer.
At first, we were inside
muted chords, inside an orgasm
of secrets, & then cried out,
Are those birds? Midnight
streetlights yellowed the snow—
a fleeting ghost battalion
cremated in the bony cages
of tanks in sand dunes. Dolphy said,
Birds have notes between our notes. . . .
I could see them among oak rafters
& beams, beyond the burning cold,
melodious in cobweb & soot.
Like false angels up there
in a war of electrical wires
& bat skeletons caked with excrement,
we in winding sheets of desire
as their unbearable songs
startled us down.

42

GUTBUCKET

I'm back, armed
with Muddy's mojo hand.
Take your daughters & hide them.
Redbuds cover the ground

like Lady Day's poppies
kissed beyond salvation & damnation:
so pretty in their Easter dresses
this day of the flower eater.

I'm fool enough to believe
loneliness can never tango me into
oblivion again. I've swayed to Lockjaw,
Trane, Pepper, & Ornette,

& outlived the cold whiteness
of Head Power in Shinjuku.
I know if you touch beauty right
a bird sings the monkey to you.

BLUE LIGHT LOUNGE SUTRA
FOR THE PERFORMANCE POETS
AT HAROLD PARK HOTEL

the need gotta be
so deep words can't
answer simple questions
all night long notes
stumble off the tongue
& color the air indigo
so deep fragments of gut
& flesh cling to the song
you gotta get into it
so deep salt crystallizes on eyelashes
the need gotta be
so deep you can vomit up ghosts
& not feel broken
'til you are no more
than a half ounce of gold
in painful brightness
you gotta get into it
blow that saxophone
so deep all the sex & dope in this world
can't erase your need
to howl against the sky
the need gotta be
so deep you can't
just wiggle your hips
& rise up out of it
chaos in the cosmos
modern man in the pepperpot
you gotta get hooked
into every hungry groove
so deep the bomb locked

in rust opens like a fist
into it into it so deep
rhythm is pre-memory
the need gotta be basic
animal need to see
& know the terror
we are made of honey
cause if you wanna dance
this boogie be ready
to let the devil use your head
for a drum.

THE STORY OF A COAT

We talked about Baroness Pannonica
driving her Silver Pigeon to the Five Spot
to chauffeur Monk home. I was happy
not to talk football, the inventory of skulls
in a cave in Somalia, the democratic vistas
of the Cedar Tavern, or about Spinoza.
We were saying how the legs go first
& then from the eyes mystery is stolen.
I said how much I miss Bill Matthews,
that sometimes at the Village Vanguard,
Fez, or Small's, especially when some cat
steals a riff out of Prez's left back pocket,
I hear his Cincinnati laugh. Then our gaze
snagged on a green dress shifting the light.
If you'd asked me, I couldn't have said why
I knew jasmine from the silence of Egypt,
or how water lives only to remember fire.
As we walked out of the sanctuary of garlic,
chive, onion, mushroom, & peppery dough,
we agreed Rahsaan could see rhythm
when he blew wounded cries of night hawks
at daybreak. The heat of the pizza parlor
followed us to the corner, & two steps later
I remembered the scent of loneliness
in my coat left draped over the chair.
I had fallen in love with its cut,
how it made me walk straighter.
When I passed the young James Dean
coming out the door with my blue-gray coat
balled up in his arms, I didn't stop him.

I don't know why. I just stood there
at the table. But, David, years after
I circled the globe, I'm still ashamed
of memories that make me American
as music made of harmony & malice.

NO·GOOD BLUES

I

I try to hide in Proust,
Mallarmé, & Camus,
but the no-good blues
come looking for me. Yeah,
come sliding in like good love
on a tongue of grease & sham,
built up from the ground.
I used to think a super-8 gearbox
did the job, that a five-hundred-dollar suit
would keep me out of Robert Johnson's
shoes. I rhyme Baudelaire
with Apollinaire, hurting
to get beyond crossroads & goofer
dust, outrunning a twelve-bar
pulsebeat. But I pick up
a hitchhiker outside Jackson.
Tasseled boots & skin-tight
jeans. You know the rest.

2

I spend winter days
with Monet, seduced
by his light. But the no-good
blues come looking for me.
It takes at least a year
to erase a scar
on a man's heart. I come home nights
drunk, the couple next door
to keep me company, their voices
undulating through my bedroom wall.
One evening I turn a corner
& step inside Bearden's "Uptown
Sunday Night Session." Faces
Armstrong blew from his horn
still hang around the Royal Gardens—all
in a few strokes, & she suddenly leans out of
a candy-apple green door & says,
Are you from Tougaloo?

3

At the Napoleon House
Beethoven's Fifth draws shadows
from the walls, & the no-good blues
come looking for me. She's here,
her left hand on my knee.
I notice a big sign
across the street that says
The Slave Exchange.
She scoots her chair closer.
I can't see betrayal
& arsenic in Napoleon's hair—
they wanted their dying emperor
under the Crescent City's
Double Scorpio. But nothing
can subdue these African voices
between the building's false floors,
this secret song from the soil
left hidden under my skin.

4

Working swing shift at McGraw-
Edison, I shoot screws
into cooler cabinets as if I were born
to do it. But the no-good blues come
looking for me. She's from Veracruz,
& never wears dead colors of the factory,
still in Frida Kahlo's world of monkeys.
She's a bird in the caged air.
The machines are bolted down
to the concrete floor,
everything moves with the same big
rhythm Mingus could get out of
a group. Humming the syncopation
of punch presses & conveyor belts,
work grows into our dance
when the foreman
hits the speed-up button
for a one-dollar bonus.

5

My hands are white
with chalk at The Emporium
in Colorado Springs, but the no-good
blues come looking for me. I miscue
when I look up & see sunlight
slanting through her dress
at the back door. That shot
costs me fifty bucks.
I let the stick glide along the V
of two fingers, knowing men who
wager their first born to conquer
snowy roller coasters & myths.
I look up, just when
the faith drains out of
my right hand. It isn't
a loose rack. But more like—
well, I know I'm in trouble
when she sinks her first ball.

6

I'm cornered at Birdland
like a two-headed man hexing
himself. But the no-good blues
come looking for me. A prayer
holds me in place,
balancing this sequined
constellation. I've hopped boxcars
& thirteen state lines to where
she stands like Ma Rainey.
Gold tooth & satin. Rotgut
& God Almighty. Moonlight
wrestling a Texas-jack.
A meteor of desire burns
my last plea to ash. Blues
don't care how many tribulations
you lay at my feet, I'll go
with you if you promise
to bring me home to Mercy.

ODE TO THE SAXOPHONE

I've heard men push their thoughts
& dreams into you, making the reed speak
& moan through your shape,
breath so close to a human voice
it says damnation & beatitude.
I know men who've kissed doubt into brass,
& heard each one say, *Life,*
tear me down to a naked sigh
on a roadside bloody with poppies.
You know, I could go on like this
'til I am kneeling before the Seventh Son.
I've heard them pour hosannahs,
field hollers, the color of a dress
turning a corner, everything into you.
Sometimes, only half of what's poured in
comes out. But I know immortality
can step into a semi-dark basement
at the 2 a.m. hour & hug a man.
I've seen them totally illuminated
or barely raised from the dead,
distant cities echoing footsteps.
All the old gospels & curses
are inside this cornucopia
of giving, & all one has to do
is turn you toward a sunset
or spotlight, up to the sky
when he's down.

CODA

Charlie, there's always another story
& this morning I'm searching again
for that photo of you & Einstein
horsing around for the Rolleiflex.
Or, maybe you're only living
in New Hope with Chan, & on the bus
reading *The New York Times,*
heading to a gig in the Big Apple.
Or the Charlie in this story is Chaplin
clowning for the camera with Albert.
Or, maybe, I'll search on the web
to see if I can buy a glimpse
of you from the other side,
while "Relaxin' At Camarillo—Take C"
fills the room. That damn photograph
is still bugging me. He's on his violin
& you're on alto. Kansas City Lightning,
man, I think you already know Monk
& Baroness Pannonica are gone, too.
They took the plaque off the house
on the corner where you used to live
across from Tompkins Square Park,
but you're still the most famous
guy on the street around here.

PART TWO

Testimony

YUSEF KOMUNYAKAA
AND SANDY EVANS

THE LIBRETTO

a day shall come
when I shall smile up
you shan't see me
but watch the blue buttercup
—Charlie Parker*

Yusef Komunyakaa's "Testimony" and the Humanity of Charlie Parker

Sascha Feinstein

If Charlie Parker could read the thousands of poems written in his honor, would he be delighted enough by the sheer volume to overlook the weakness of the verse itself? Perhaps. He was known, after all, for his generous praise, and certainly one cannot fault the inspiration for these poems, Parker being one of the most important artists of the twentieth (or any) century. As most people know, he spearheaded the modern jazz movement in the forties, actively changing the language of music in terms of harmonic structure, musical cadence, melodic lines, and velocity. (Parker's well-known involvement with narcotics made him all the more popular; he represented the ultimate in hipster mystique: frantic genius, coupled with romanticized overindulgence.) When he died in 1955 at the age of thirty-four, poets across the country tried to express the depth of their loss, gratitude, and awe. Scrawled napkins in coffeehouses, academic journal publications, spray-painted slogans on cement walls—tributes to Bird inundated the American landscape. But how many of these poems from the fifties to the present deserve a lengthy discussion? Sadly, very few.

I do not mean to dismiss some exceptional pieces by writers such as Bob Kaufman, Ted Joans, Owen Dodson, Larry Neal, Jack Spicer, Amiri Baraka, Jayne Cortez, Michael Harper, and, more recently, Christopher Gilbert, Joy Harjo, Lynda Hull, Paul Zimmer, Betsy Sholl, Dionisio D. Martínez, and others. This is a sincere qualification; over the last fifty years, a number of fine writers have produced excellent Bird poems. Still, the vast majority of Parker homages rely on clichés, most obviously "Bird lives!" but also "Blow, Bird, blow!" as well as a host of dreadful ornithological metaphors. Humbled by Parker's mythic legacy, poets tended to praise him with embarrassingly hagiographic detail, equating him to Christ, Buddha, and other gods and saints. In verse, he was always Bird, but rarely Charles.

Which is why we should be all the more grateful for Yusef Komunyakaa's "Testimony," a fourteen-page libretto that explores the life and legacy of Charlie Parker. The longest jazz-related poem of Komunyakaa's career, "Testimony" achieves what so many other poems do not: it celebrates Parker's humanity, and in doing so, it does not shy from the complexity of his music or personality. The poem encounters Parker at various stages of the alto saxophonist's life and presents a variety of voices that broaden our perspectives on the man and his music. Komunyakaa testifies to genius but never at the expense of human truths, nor does he allow biography to eclipse his own artistry: stanza by stanza, section after section, he fuses language and music with astonishing success.

Komunyakaa wrote "Testimony" on commission for ABC radio in Australia. The poem first appeared in *Brilliant Corners: A Journal of Jazz & Literature,* accompanied by an interview that focused on the work. Later, "Testimony" showed up in his collection *Thieves of Paradise* (Wesleyan University Press, 1998). Four years later, in January 2002, two-dozen musicians and singers performed the libretto at Sydney's Opera House. Wildly enthusiastic reviews described the performance as a visual and aural extravaganza, and reading the poem on the page cannot quite compete with a multitiered stage and gigantic screens with bright slideshows of Charlie Parker, nor does the reader experience the immediacy of hearing an alto saxophone. Yet on the page, we experience a more intimate relationship—at least in terms of the narrative—between Charlie Parker and Komunyakaa's complex exploration of history and sound. "I think with Bird's alto," Komunyakaa said in a *Brilliant Corners* interview, "there's a great lyricism, almost a tonal narrative. I'm also interested in the fact that he had such an intricate relationship with the blues—and a blues is not always a dirge. [Grins.] There's wonderment. There's laughter. There's a wholeness to his vision that I admire, and a bravery as well."[1] With or without musical accompaniment, however, this libretto testifies to the breadth of Parker's legacy more than any other individual poem.

The first section of "Testimony" depicts Parker's early years, leading to "a slow Greyhound / headed for the Big Apple / . . . [while] 'Honeysuckle Rose' / blossomed into body language, / driven by a sunset on the Hudson." By the second section, Parker is already the consummate artist, "Washing dishes at Jimmy's / Chicken Shack . . . / just to hear Art Tatum." We also witness his revelatory moment playing the tune "Cherokee," when, as the poem tells us, "he could finally play / everything inside his head" and "was ready to squeeze / elevenths, thirteenths, / every silent grace note / of blood into each dream / he dared to play." These opening passages present pivotal episodes in Parker's early career, establishing first his profound desire to learn, and then his breakthrough as a young artist.

Biographically, these opening sections, and many others that follow, borrow from established sources, chiefly Gary Giddins's *Celebrating Bird: The Triumph of Charlie Parker*,[2] an excellent study. Virtually all the allusions to Parker's life in "Testimony"—and readers unfamiliar with jazz will find many genuinely obscure—can be tracked down in Giddins's extremely compact biography. *Celebrating Bird* also includes a splendid gathering of photographs that dramatically influenced the poem, particularly two childhood portraits of Parker (in one, he's sitting beside his half brother; in another, he's riding a pony) as well as the final photograph in the book (a detail of Parker's engraved alto). But Komunyakaa's poem, of course, sounds nothing like Giddins's prose, and the strength of "Testimony" relies much less on biography than poetry. (Compare this poem to Martin Gray's *Blues for Bird*, a book-length poem that reads like merely chopped-up, standard prose.) Parker's epiphanic experience playing "Cherokee," for example, remains a well-known episode in jazz history, but Komunyakaa invigorates the moment with language evocative enough to tease our own imagination: liberated, Parker could suddenly feel "the melodic line modulating / through his bones to align itself / with Venus & the Dog Star."

By grounding the poem in Sections I and II with biography, Komunyakaa places the reader squarely in a specific historical context, a framework within which he can meditate on the aesthetics of jazz. In Section III, one that should be quoted in its entirety, Komunyakaa transforms the music and sensibilities of Parker into a dazzling portrait of color:

Purple dress. Midnight-blue.
Dime-store floral print
blouse draped over a Botticellian
pose. Tangerine. He could blow
insinuation. A train whistle
in the distance, gun shot
through the ceiling, a wood warbler
back in the Ozarks at Lake
Taneycomo, he'd harmonize
them all. Celt dealing in coal
on the edge of swing. Blue
dress. Carmine. Yellow sapsucker,
bodacious *zoot suit with the reet*
pleats & shim sham shimmy.

Lime-green skirt. Black silk
petticoat. Velveteen masterpiece &
mindreader twirling like a spotlight
on the dance floor. Yardbird
could blow a woman's strut
across the room. "Alice in
Blue" & "The Lady in Red"
pushed moans through brass.
Mink-collared cashmere & pillbox.
Georgia peach. Pearlized facade
& foxtrot. Vermillion dress. High
heels clicking like a high hat.
Black-beaded flapper. Blue satin.
Yardbird, he'd blow pain & glitter.

"It's interesting," Komunyakaa explained, "that idea of Parker being associated with visual arts. Colors and textures. Textured motion and emotion. . . . The idea of blowing colors is interesting to me, and I do think that there are certain tones that parallel certain colors." Although the reader does not necessarily hear Bird in these colors (how would that be possible?), the painterly descriptions suggest the lavish qualities of great music. While the passage praises Parker's ability to play "insinuation," the section itself insinuates jazz.

The use of multiple voices also distinguishes this poem from so many other efforts, and these varying perspectives allow for vocal textures in the verse, while at the same time broadening the portraiture. As Komunyakaa noted, "Testimony" features "people telling different stories, or, at times, telling riffs on the same stories." We hear reports from several musicians whose narratives differ dramatically and who, therefore, afford new ways of understanding Parker. Sometimes, the individual report provides a wide swath of information. In Section V, for example, Bird appears as an intellectual, hip to current events ("Bird talked Lenny / before Bruce was heard of"), and as an irresistible trickster figure:

> Maybe it was sunny or cloudy
> with our tears, like other days
> when Max's mama slid her key
> into the front-door lock. Bird
> would jump up, grab the Bible
> & start thumbing through pages,
> & Mrs. Roach would say, *Why*
> *aren't you all more like Charlie?*

In Section VI a piano player reflects on personal experiences, but here the portrait addresses the politics of race—and not the standard politics, either:

> Now, you
> take Ikey, Charlie's half-brother
> by an Italian woman, their father
> would take him from friend
> to friend, saying, *He's got good*
> *hair.*

At this point, the voice changes to the speaker's commentary:

> Is this why Charlie
> would hide under his bed & play
> dead 'til his mother kissed him
> awake? No wonder he lived
> like a floating rib
> in a howl whispered through brass.

Typical of Komunyakaa's work in general, these passages understate explosive scenes and encourage the reader to meditate on painful details, realities that extend far beyond the life of Charlie Parker and that cause the verse to resonate all the more.

We hear from an anonymous speaker who knew Bird in childhood, and we hear from Baroness Pannonica de Koenigswarter, in whose apartment Parker died. (Her attacks against the media prove how little Americans have changed in terms of sensitivity, privacy, and good judgment.) And we hear from Parker himself—those devastating telegrams from Los Angeles to his wife in New York, telegrams responding to their daughter's death and written, as Komunyakaa explained, "almost as though he's forgotten the previous line, like words strung together by pain and regret":

> *My daughter is dead.*
> *I will be there as quick*
> *as I can. My name is Bird.*
> *It is very nice to be out here.*
> *I am coming in right away.*
> *Take it easy. Let me be the first*
> *one to approach you. I am*
> *your husband. Sincerely,*
> *Charlie Parker.*

The speaker responds:

Now, don't
say we can't already hear
those telegraph keys playing Bartok
'til the mockingbird loses its tongue,
already playing Pree's funeral song
from the City of Angels.

By the end of "Testimony," we have witnessed Charlie Parker through many sets of eyes. "Everyone," the poem tells us, "has a Bird story." Typical of Komunyakaa's poetic grace, as well as his remarkably humble nature, he allows others to speak on his behalf while at the same time enhancing their voices with his own imaginative observations and stunning lyricism.

And after that kind of exhaustive coverage, the poem moves naturally to the diaspora of myth: Parker's legacy. The final section simultaneously embraces the strange mythos of Bird and celebrates his genius in a way that makes him absolutely present in our world, half a century later:

Someone spoke about a letter
in *Down Beat* from a G.I.
in Korea who stole back
a recording of "Bird in Paradise"
from a dead Chinese soldier's hand.
Someone counted the letters in his name
& broke the bagman's bank. Maybe
there's something to all this
talk about seeing a graven image
of Bird in Buddha & the Sphinx.
Although half of the root's gone,
heavy with phantom limbs, French
flowers engraved into his horn
bloom into the after-hours.

Although the poem refers to Buddha, it does not insist upon dramatic parallels. Instead, Komunyakaa acknowledges that "something" spiritual might indeed be at the base of superficial "talk." In fact, the poem's close functions similarly: with a conscious dismissal of the standard line, "Bird lives!" Instead, Yusef Komunyakaa replaces a cliché with real poetry, transforming the filigree from Parker's Selmer saxophone into an organic metaphor that suggests Charlie Parker's sustained legacy.

NOTES

1. Yusef Komunyakaa's words are from the 1997 *Brilliant Corners* interview, "Survival Masks: Yusef Komunyakaa with Sascha Feinstein," which follows.

2. Giddens, Gary. *Celebrating Bird: The Triumph of Charlie Parker,* New York: De Capo Press, 1998.

Survival Masks

AN INTERVIEW WITH YUSEF KOMUNYAKAA

Sascha Feinstein

This interview took place at The Runcible Spoon, a coffeehouse in Bloomington, Indiana on June 25th, 1997.

Sascha Feinstein: What initially inspired you to write a libretto?

Yusef Komunyakaa: Well, Chris Williams at the Australian Broadcasting Corporation first approached me in early 1995 with the idea of a libretto, something that celebrated jazz's relationship with blues and gospel. I chimed to this wonderful idea because I feel that my work, my poetry, has evolved out of this musical tradition. In this first discussion, Chris described his admiration for Charlie Parker's musical ideas and then he mentioned that most likely Sandy Evans would compose the music.

Immediately I felt this was a healthy challenge. I had heard one of her three groups, Ten Part Invention, at a local pub a week earlier in Sydney and I remembered going away highly impressed. She has exciting musical ideas, and she blows that sax as if she was made for the instrument. However, the more I thought about the impending piece, the more I wanted to write something new and different. I began to play Charlie Parker, everything he did, and I clothed my psyche in his sounds again. Though I'd listened to him through the years, he was still new and traditional in the same breath, old and cosmopolitan.

I think Chris was thinking of a more traditional libretto but I wanted a flexible definition. With Parker, I felt that a traditional libretto would pull against his experimentation and his whole trajectory of working things out as he went along. I wanted the piece to emulate the musical ideas, how they would flow for him.

Feinstein: In essence, what did you keep and what did you pull away from?

Komunyakaa: I pulled away from the structure of the libretto. I wanted something to excite me and surprise me, so what I went for was a kind of composite. I started thinking about the actions of Parker, and also about the fact that many of the stories were erroneous, misleading. A good example is the story that Parker died in Baroness Pannonica's bathroom at the Stanhope Hotel with a needle in his arm. This is the story I had been told. So everything was rather melodramatic and less complex, and what I wanted to do was capture the complexity of this man.

Feinstein: Of course, the truth of his death—that he died watching a juggler on the TV—has often become melodramatic in the way that it's been presented and reported.

Komunyakaa: Yes, right. But at least there's something pleasing about the truth. Let's face it, he's *laughing,* and not sitting on the commode grimacing with a needle in his arm.

Feinstein: I know that often in your career a particular poem has triggered many others, even an entire book. Did a particular section or image generate the rest of this poem?

Komunyakaa: I tell you, the first idea that came to me was based on a photograph I'd seen of Parker where he's about one year, holding a brush in his hand. There's something about the severe innocence.

Feinstein: He looks like a girl.

Komunyakaa: Yes, very much so. I kept glancing from that photo to the photo of him at the Bird's Nest in Los Angeles in 1947. He's with Harold Doc West, Red Callender and Erroll Garner, and he has a smile that suggests he has been initiated by hard times and joy. It is a visual moment of knowledge and acknowledgment. Cocky.

And, also, there's another photograph of Parker as a young boy, maybe a year and a half, astride a Palomino pony. I began to weight this image against the image of him carefully listening to two Apache visitors, Swift Eagle and Bad Wolf, at the Royal Roost. He seems so attentive, it parallels something glimpsed of him in those early images. I wanted to at least attempt to unearth a moment of this somethingness, this mystery, through "Testimony." But I was also drawn to the later photographs of Parker. So

I am interested in that contrast—the innocence and, later on, something close to a visual ferocity.

We tend to think of jazz and gospel as opposites. Blues is called "the Devil's music." One is secular, the other sacred. I tend to think of Parker as blowing both at the same time. I feel that the technology of sound through brass is his religion.

Feinstein: Obviously the music itself was the primary influence on your poem, but you also address biographical issues. Were there any literary sources that you found helpful?

Komunyakaa: I've read a number of works on Parker, such as Ross Russell's *Bird Lives!*

Feinstein: Which in fact takes many liberties with the truth—

Komunyakaa: That's the first one I read. Then I went to [Gary] Giddins' *Celebrating Bird* and Robert Reisner's *The Legend of Charlie Parker*—even to liner notes [especially Phil Schaap's writing for *Bird: The Complete Charlie Parker on Verve*], which are quite informative as well. So it was all of those things plus the imagination. I tried to create an emotional composite of the man.

Feinstein: I love how you make the effort to talk both about his life and the aesthetics of jazz, and my favorite section may very well be the third, with all the lush colors.

Komunyakaa: It's interesting, that idea of Parker being associated with visual arts. Colors and textures. Textured motion and emotion. I believe many visual artists have been influenced by jazz and the atmosphere it creates. I am thinking about Romare Bearden, Matisse's "Jazz" series, Otto Dix, Picasso, and so forth. Recently I saw an exhibit and I was quite taken with the fact there were so many visual images of Armstrong—literally hundreds—and there must be hundreds of Parker as well. I know at least one sculpture that captures him in stone, a piece by Julie MacDonald.

The idea of blowing colors is interesting to me, and I do think that there are certain tones that parallel certain colors. In a sense, that's the way I approach poetry. I think I've said somewhere that I wish I were a visual artist at times.

Feinstein: Many poets have said that.

Komunyakaa: Right. [Laughs.] The very first time someone asked me, "How do you define your poetry?" I remember saying, "I think they're word paintings." In a certain sense, I think of Parker's tunes as pictorial.

Feinstein: "Testimony" seems to have changes in speaker. Do you hear vocal shifts?

Komunyakaa: I see this as many speakers, people telling different stories, or, at times, telling riffs on the same stories. Dealing with the space, I couldn't do *too* much of that. But this again emphasizes the complexity of Parker. I wanted a few of the pieces as multiple voices, with two or three people talking. I also wanted to give room to the director, where he could deal with these different voices. I think what Chris has planned so far is to use a thirteen piece band and two actors, and a male chorus of four voices. So I kept thinking, "How would I do it?" and in certain cases I could see bringing in another voice in the middle of an idea or sentence.

This sort of parallels the way I construct poems often, in the sense that I love the idea of shifts happening where things are not completely resolved, where narratives do not necessarily have a lineal chart or continuity. In that way it parallels the idea of the psyche where there are many shifts.

Let's face it, Parker would have observed all kinds of things. He was a very troubled man, growing up in the Midwest, traveling around America and Europe, never really making much money, always living on the edge. But at the same time, I've seen so many photographs of him smiling—one where he's smelling a flower—which is interesting to me.

Feinstein: William Claxton selected the photograph that will be on the cover of this issue [Winter 1997] because he said he never caught Parker looking happier.

Komunyakaa: Parker seemed capable of being happy in the most troublesome moments, and I think that is the energy that people often relate to when they say "Bird" and give him this sacred dimension. I'm thinking of that Jack Kerouac poem ["239th Chorus" from *Mexico City Blues*] where he attempts to elevate Parker to Buddhahood. Parker had this capacity of embracing others, and at the same time he appears as a

Trickster—trying to survive his habit, on the edge. But I don't think he ever tricked himself.

He wore many masks, multiple masks. I would classify them mainly as survival masks more than anything else. I don't know if he grew up lonely, but maybe he began creating survival masks early on, within the context of his family.

Feinstein: In the 1950s, poets dispersed Bird poems like napkins. [Komunyakaa laughs.] Some poets were much more successful than others, and I remember a few years ago when you said that Bob Kaufman had been an influential figure on your [early] poetry. Kaufman, of course, was almost obsessively attracted to Parker.

Komunyakaa: To the extent that he even named his son "Parker."

Feinstein: Do you still feel his presence guiding your sensibilities as a poet?

Komunyakaa: I'm not as quirky as Bob Kaufman. At times I wish I were! [Laughs.] He's full of surprises, and the other thing is his obsession: there's a body to that obsession which propels the music of the poems. You see that in Parker as well. I'm still quite taken with Kaufman, with his obsessive imagination.

Feinstein: You can tell that he really listened, and that he genuinely loved Charlie Parker as a human being and as an artist.

Komunyakaa: He respected Parker.

Feinstein: I think Kaufman's poems for Bird [compared to many others from the '50s] were most in tune with Parker's spirit.

Komunyakaa: Yes. He was able to penetrate the internal terrain, to get to the essence of Bird, the man. Maybe he saw part of himself in Parker. I don't know if I see part of myself in Kaufman, but it's interesting that Kaufman grew up in Louisiana [as I did], born into a complex family, with a black mother and Jewish father.

Feinstein: Many of Kaufman's contemporaries who tried to write Bird poems were, I think, emotionally removed from Parker. How did you solve that problem?

Komunyakaa: I really had to find myself meditating on the essence of Bird, and I'm glad I didn't attempt these poems early on—say, fifteen years ago. I don't know if I understood Bird early on, and I think it takes a certain amount of maturity to understand where Bird is coming from. I had to understand important things about myself in order to understand Bird. I was able to place myself, at times, in his situation. And at first it was terrifying, because people often talk about Bird and his habit.

Feinstein: Which, needless to say, did not literally parallel your life.

Komunyakaa: Of course. But I do empathize with him and understand how history helped to create him. I think he was more tender than he often wanted to appear—as hard edged as possible (maybe because he grew up in Kansas City). I was taken by the fact that Bird would wash dishes at Jimmy's Chicken Shack just to hear Art Tatum.

I think with Bird's alto there's a great lyricism, almost a tonal narrative. I'm also interested in the fact that he had such an intricate relationship with the blues—and a blues is not always a dirge. [Grins.] There's wonderment. There's laughter. There's a wholeness to his vision that I admire, and a bravery as well. There's also an ego he constantly wrestles with in his work.

Feinstein: The title of your poem changed several times.

Komunyakaa: Originally, Chris [Williams] suggested the title "Call and Response," and this idea of call and response as a dramatic device still interests me of course. Then it changed to "Séance," but there's something about "séance" that didn't work because there's this idea of conjuring the dead. But "Testimony" is a kind of coming forth, telling a story—a number of stories, contradictions—braided into the fabric and design of the piece. At the same time, it's a celebration.

Feinstein: Bringing emotional extremes together has been a central concern of yours throughout your career as a poet, and this poem certainly does that, sometimes quite directly: "Maybe that's when he first / played laughter & crying / at the same time." And that's also at the center of the blues.

Komunyakaa: Yes. I think so.

Feinstein: Did you ever have an experience in your life that was similar to Parker's artistic breakthrough when playing "Cherokee"?

Komunyakaa: That's an interesting question. When I went to Irvine in

1978 after living in Colorado for seven-and-a-half years, I wrote a poem called "Safe Subjects," and after writing that poem I realized there was something that taught me what I should try to accomplish in my work. It really became a directive: "Let truth have its way with us / like a fishhook holds / to life, holds dearly to nothing / worth saying"

Feinstein: You've said before that you'll start a poem with a refrain and then later extract it. I'm so glad you left the repetition in "Section V."

Komunyakaa: It's a riff on how stories come about, on possibilities.

Feinstein: What made you bring in [Anatole] Broyard [in Section V]?

Komunyakaa: I wanted something to complicate the situation, and I visualized Broyard walking through Washington Square Park, actually going past Bird. I think Parker was very aware of race, even in relation to his half-brother, Ikey.

Feinstein: Those issues certainly arise in Section VI. And I love that image of Bird being awakened by his mother's kisses.

Komunyakaa: When you think about it, the two brothers become a metaphor for the tensions of race in America, with Parker as a child hiding under the bed.

Perhaps it was that tension of growing up in the 1920s that helped to create the lyrical tension beneath Parker's alto. In Amiri Baraka's *Dutchman,* the character Clay says that Yardbird wouldn't have played with such urgency if he had gone out into the streets and killed a white person. (Of course, this existential act in *Dutchman* echoes Richard Wright's *Native Son.*) Indeed, I feel muted screams underneath Parker's lyricism. There's a rage just below the surface of a blues tonality that has been created out of need. He is sensitive to what is happening around him and to him.

Feinstein: Where did you first encounter the telegrams [in Section X] that he sends to [his wife] Chan after their daughter's death?

Komunyakaa: I don't even recall when I first encountered them. Maybe they are in Robert Reisner's *The Legend of Charlie Parker.* I do remember feeling that a cry sounded through the room as I read them. There's a quiet desperation in those telegrams—quiet because of the words chosen, but at the same time there's something frantic about them as well.

Feinstein: Phrase against phrase.

Komunyakaa: One after the other, almost as though he's forgotten the previous line, like words strung together by pain and regret.

Feinstein: And those strange signatures, "Sincerely, your husband."

Komunyakaa: Yes—almost as if he had to remind himself, out in L.A. I don't think he ever got along too well in L.A., that he was more at home in New York. He suffered in L.A. and found himself doing bizarre things.

Feinstein: At what point in making "Testimony" did you visualize the wondrous final images of the Chinese soldier and the engravings on Parker's horn?

Komunyakaa: That came to me as a breakthrough. One of the agonies of writing poetry is the question, "Where am I going to end this poem?" But midway through I started writing about the soldier, and the horn. For some reason I put that aside and then got back to it close to the end, and said, "Yes. This is the ending." It surprised me, and I do think it is the right stroke on the canvas.

Feinstein: "Testimony" is an individual section of your book, *Thieves of Paradise,* which has seven sections. How does the poem function in this context?

Komunyakaa: It functions as a bridge. I think it's different from anything else in the book, and I'm glad that it's different because it sort of switches gears, but the emotional trajectory isn't broken.

Feinstein: Switching gears from what?

Komunyakaa: I think the subject matter's different, more urban. There are many shifts in "Testimony" that have to do with the possibility of many voices. Tonally it's different, though it's hard to say how exactly.

Feinstein: That's all right. Let other people chew the fat over those questions. [Komunyakaa laughs.] "Testimony" may very well be the longest poem you've ever written. Did you find the length liberating?

Komunyakaa: I had to surrender to its structure. I knew I wanted symmetry—not as a mold but as an organizing principle—and it liberated me in that sense. Two fourteen-lined stanzas. Fourteen sections. I seem to always get involved with numerology and destiny.

Feinstein: And you chose fourteen because—?

Komunyakaa: You can divide seven into fourteen twice. [Laughs.] Often this becomes an obsession of sorts, what I call an emotional symmetry.

Feinstein: There's a knockout line break in Section VIII: "Wearing nothing but sky- / blue socks." That break on the hyphen is quite unusual for you. [Komunyakaa grins.] You often avoid breaks that might be seen as almost too clever—that bring attention to themselves. But I think it works marvelously well here.

Komunyakaa: For a long time, that was the very first image [in the poem] for me. And for some reason, when I initially wrote it, the break was there, and I kept it.

Feinstein: There's a truth to that image.

Komunyakaa: I hope so.

Feinstein: And I admire the way you address his stay at Camarillo [State Hospital] not merely as an emotional breakdown but also as a more positive revelation.

Komunyakaa: I was quite taken with the fact he experienced so much pleasure getting his hands into the dirt. It says something about Parker, and in a way it takes him back to his beginnings. For years I thought of the Midwest as restrictive and reactionary, but recently I've been having this idea about all the experimentation that came out of that part of the country.

So I could see Parker embracing a certain kind of space early on. It might even have something to do with his creative dexterity, you know? He was able to move from one musical idea to the next, and to embrace different people and musical situations. I think it has everything to do with the fact that physical space parallels emotional and psychological space. He was at home.

TESTIMONY

I

He hopped boxcars to Chitown
late fall, just a few steps
ahead of the hawk. After
sleepwalking to the 65 Club,
he begged Goon for a chance
to sit in with a borrowed sax.
He'd paid his dues for years
blowing ravenous after-hours
'til secrets filled with blues
rooted in Mississippi mud;
he confessed to Budd Johnson
that as a boy playing stickball,
sometimes he'd spy in a window
as they rehearsed back in K. C.

It was Goon who took him home,
gave him clothes & a clarinet.
Maybe that's when he first
played laughter & crying
at the same time. Nights
sucked the day's marrow
'til the hibernating moon grew
fat with lies & chords. Weeks
later, with the horn hocked,
he was on a slow Greyhound
headed for the Big Apple,
& "Honeysuckle Rose"
blossomed into body language,
driven by a sunset on the Hudson.

Washing dishes at Jimmy's
Chicken Shack from midnight
to eight for nine bucks a week
just to hear Art Tatum's keys,
he simmered in jubilation
for over three months. After
a tango palace in Times Square
& jam sessions at Clark Monroe's,
in the back room of a chili house
on "Cherokee," he could finally play
everything inside his head,
the melodic line modulating
through his bones to align itself
with Venus & the Dog Star.

Some lodestone pulled him
to Banjo's show band on the highway
'til Baltimore hexed him: a train
ticket & a telegram said a jealous
lover stabbed his father to death.
He followed a spectral cologne
'til he was back with Hootie,
'til that joke about chickens
hit by a car swelled into legend.
Now, he was ready to squeeze
elevenths, thirteenths,
every silent grace note
of blood into each dream
he dared to play.

Purple dress. Midnight-blue.
Dime-store floral print
blouse draped over a Botticellian
pose. Tangerine. He could blow
insinuation. A train whistle
in the distance, gun shot
through the ceiling, a wood warbler
back in the Ozarks at Lake
Taneycomo, he'd harmonize
them all. Celt dealing in coal
on the edge of swing. Blue
dress. Carmine. Yellow sapsucker,
bodacious *zoot suit with the reet
pleats* & shim sham shimmy.

Lime-green skirt. Black silk
petticoat. Velveteen masterpiece &
mindreader twirling like a spotlight
on the dance floor. Yardbird
could blow a woman's strut
across the room. "Alice in
Blue" & "The Lady in Red"
pushed moans through brass.
Mink-collared cashmere & pillbox.
Georgia peach. Pearlized façade
& foxtrot. Vermillion dress. High
heels clicking like a high hat.
Black-beaded flapper. Blue satin.
Yardbird, he'd blow pain & glitter.

Moving eastward to the Deep
South with Jay McShann,
on trains whistling into dogwood
& pine, past shadows dragging balls
& chains, Bird landed in jail
in Jackson for lollygagging
on the front porch of a boardinghouse
with the lights on. For two days
he fingered a phantom alto
'til "What Price Love" spoke
through metal & fluted bone.
The band roared through the
scent of mayhaw & muscadine,
back into Chicago & Detroit.

When the truckload of horns
& drums rolled into Manhattan,
Bird slid behind the wheel.
The three-car caravan
followed, looping Central Park
'til a mounted policeman
brandished his handcuffs.
Days later, after moving into the Woodside,
after a battery of cutting contests,
Ben Webster heard them & ran downtown
to Fifty-second Street & said
they were kicking in the devil's door
& putting the night back
together up at the Savoy.

V

Maybe it was a day like today.
We sat in Washington Square Park
sipping wine from a Dixie cup
when Bird glimpsed Anatole
Broyard walking past & said,
He's one of us, but he doesn't
want to admit he's one of us.
Maybe it was only guesswork
contorted into breath. We sat
staring after Anatole until he
disappeared down Waverly Place.
Bird took a sip, shook his head,
& said, *Now, that guy chases*
heartbreak more than I do.

Maybe it was a day like today.
We were over at Max's house
as Bird talked Lenny
before Bruce was heard of,
telling a story about a club owner's
parrot squawking the magic word.
Maybe it was sunny or cloudy
with our tears, like the other days
when Max's mama slid her key
into the front-door lock. Bird
would jump up, grab the Bible
& start thumbing through pages,
& Mrs. Roach would say, *Why*
aren't you all more like Charlie?

If you favor your left
hand over the right, one
turns into Abel & the other
into Cain. Now, you
take Ikey, Charlie's half-brother
by an Italian woman, their father
would take him from friend
to friend, saying, *He's got good*
hair. Is this why Charlie
would hide under his bed & play
dead 'til his mother kissed him
awake? No wonder he lived
like a floating rib
in a howl whispered through brass.

Always on the move, Charlie
traversed the heart's nine rings
from the Ozarks to le Boeuf
sur le Toit in Montmartre.
Though he never persuaded himself
to stay overseas, his first day
in Stockholm glowed among fallen
shadows. Always on some no-man's
land, he'd close his eyes
& fly to that cluster of Swedes
as he spoke of his favorite artist:
Heifetz cried through his violin.
Charlie could be two places at once,
always arm-wrestling himself in the dark.

Like a black cockatoo
clinging to a stormy branch
with its shiny head rocking
between paradise & hell,
that's how Yardbird
listened. He'd go inside
a song with enough irony
to break the devil's heart.
Listening with his whole body,
he'd enter the liquid machine
of cow bells & vibes,
of congas & timbales,
& when he'd raise his alto
a tropic sun beamed into the club.

Machito & his Afro-Cuban
Orchestra peppered the night
'til Yardbird left ash in the bell
of his horn. He swore Africa
swelled up through the soles
of his feet, that a Latin beat
would start like the distant
knocking of tiny rods & pistons
'til he found himself mamboing.
He must've known this is
the same feeling that drives
sap through mango leaves,
up into the fruit's sweet
flesh & stony pit.

He was naked,
wearing nothing but sky-
blue socks in the lobby
of the Civic Hotel in Little Tokyo,
begging for a quarter
to make a phone call. The Chinese
manager led him back to his room,
but minutes later a whiff of smoke
trailed him down the staircase.
This was how six yellow pills
sobered him up for a recording
session. He was naked, & now
as firemen extinguished the bed
cops wrestled him into a straitjacket.

Camarillo's oceanic sky opened
over his head for sixteen months
when the judge's makeshift bench
rolled away from his cell door.
Eucalyptus trees guarded this
dreamtime. Yardbird loved
working his hands into the soil
'til heads of lettuce grew round
& fat as the promises he made
to himself, lovers, & friends.
Saturday nights he'd blow
a C-melody sax so hard
he'd gaze into the eyes of the other patients
to face a naked mirror again.

I can see him, a small boy
clutching a hairbrush.
This is 8 5 2 Freeman
Street, just after his father
took off on the Pullman line
with a porter's jacket
flapping like a white flag.
A few years later, he's astride
a palomino on Oliver Street
where a potbellied stove
glowed red-hot as a nightclub
down the block. Rudee Vallee
& late nights on Twelfth
haven't marked him yet.

When I think of Bird, bad
luck hasn't seethed into his body,
& Kansas City isn't Tom's
Town. This is before the silver
Conn bought on time, before Rebecca's
mother rented the second-floor,
before prophecies written on his back
at the Subway Club by Buster & Prez
on "Body & Soul," long before
Jo Jones threw those cymbals
at his feet, before benzedrine
capsules in rotgut & the needle's
first bite, before he was bittersweet
as April, when he was still Addie's boy.

X

My darling. My daughter's death
surprised me more than it did you.
Don't fulfill funeral proceeding until
I get there. I shall be the first
one to walk into our chapel.
Forgive me for not being there
with you while you were at
the hospital. Yours most sincerely,
your husband, Charlie Parker.
Now, don't say you can't hear
Bird crying inside these words
from L.A. to New York,
trying to ease Chan's pain,
trying to save himself.

My daughter is dead.
I will be there as quick
as I can. My name is Bird.
It is very nice to be out here.
I am coming in right away.
Take it easy. Let me be the first
one to approach you. I am
your husband. Sincerely,
Charlie Parker. Now, don't
say we can't already hear
those telegraph keys playing Bartok
'til the mockingbird loses its tongue,
already playing Pree's funeral song
from the City of Angels.

I believe a bohemian girl
took me to Barrow Street
to one of those dress-up parties
where nobody's feet touched
the floor. I know it was months
after they barred Bird
from Birdland. Months
after he drank iodine,
trying to devour one hundred
black roses. Ted Joans
& Basheer also lived there,
sleeping three in a bed
to keep warm. A woman dusted
a powdered mask on Bird's face.

I remember he couldn't stop
talking about Dali & Beethoven,
couldn't stop counting up gigs
as if tallying losses: the Argyle . . .
Bar de Duc . . . the Bee Hive . . .
Chanticleer . . . Club de Lisa . . .
El Grotto Room . . . Greenleaf Gardens . . .
Hi De Ho . . . Jubilee Junction . . .
Le Club Downbeat . . . Lucille's Band Box . . .
The Open Door . . . St. Nick's . . . Storyville.
I remember some hepcat talking about
vaccinated bread, & then Bird began
cussing out someone inside his head
called Moose the Mooche. I remember.

Bird was a pushover, a soft
touch for strings, for the low
& the high, for sonorous catgut
& the low-down plucked ecstasy
of garter belts. He loved
strings. A medley of nerve endings
ran through every earth color: sky
to loam, rainbow to backbone
strung like harp & cello.
But he never wrung true blues
out of those strings, couldn't
weave the vibrato of syncopated
brass & ghosts
'til some naked thing cried out.

Double-hearted instruments breathed
beneath light wood, but no real flesh
& blood moaned into that unbruised
surrender. Did he think Edgard
Varese & Stefan Wolpe could help
heal the track marks crisscrossing
veins that worked their way back
up the Nile & down the Tigris?
Stravinsky & Prokofiev. Bird
loved strings. Each loveknot
& chord stitched a dream to scar
tissue. But he knew if he plucked
the wrong one too hard, someday a nightmare
would break & fall into his hands.

They asked questions so hard
they tried to hook the heart
& yank it through the mouth.
I smiled. They shifted
their feet & stood there
with hats in hands, hurting
for headlines: *Baroness Pannonica* . . .
I told them how I met my husband
at Le Touquet airport, about decoding
for De Gaulle, about my coming-out ball.
I said I heard a thunderclap,
but they didn't want to hear
how Charlie died laughing
at jugglers on the Dorsey show.

The Stanhope buzzed with innuendo.
Yes, they had him with a needle
in his arm dead in my bathroom.
They loved to hear me say that
he was so sick he refused a shot
of gin. I told them his body
arrived at Bellevue five hours
later, tagged John Parker.
I told them how I wandered
around the Village in circles,
running into old friends,
that a cry held down my tongue
'til I found Chan, but they only
wanted us nude in bed together.

They wanted to hold his Selmer,
to put lips to the mouthpiece,
to have their pictures snapped
beneath *Bird Lives! Bird Lives!*
scrawled across Village walls
& subway trains. Three women
sang over his body, but no one read
The Rubaiyat of Omar Khayyam
aloud. Two swore he never said
Please don't let them bury me
in Kansas City. Everyone
has a Bird story. Someone
said he wished for the words
Bird recited for midnight fixes.

Someone spoke about a letter
in *Down Beat* from a G.I.
in Korea who stole back
a recording of "Bird in Paradise"
from a dead Chinese soldier's hand.
Someone counted the letters in his name
& broke the bagman's bank. Maybe
there's something to all this
talk about seeing a graven image
of Bird in Buddha & the Sphinx.
Although half of the root's gone,
heavy with phantom limbs, French
flowers engraved into his horn
bloom into the after-hours.

I'll never make that again.
—Charlie Parker*

*Charlie Parker to Ross Russell, recording
Night in Tunisia, 1947. Ross Russell, "Sympo-
sium Keynote Address," *The Bebop Revolution
in Words and Music,* Dave Oliphant, ed.
Harry Ransom Humanities Research Center,
The University of Texas at Austin, 1994.

Testimony, The Ties that Bind
Miriam Zolin

One story you hear around these parts is that in the 1950s a teenage John Pochée used to ask his mother for bus money so he could visit the late Joe 'Bebop' Lane and listen to Lane's copy of a Charlie Parker record—one of a rare few that had made their way across the world to this faraway island continent of Australia. Ten years younger than Lane, Pochée later became co-founder of super-band Ten Part Invention, and has been a longtime collaborator with alto saxophonist Bernie McGann—one of the key voices Sandy Evans chose to feature in *Testimony.*

John Clare in *Bodgie Dada and the Cult of Cool* relates stories from the same era in Sydney, backyard gatherings of enthusiastic young players and even the adoption of a hip "jazz talk" among a group for whom this music represented liberation, "something we couldn't even talk about" (quoting David Tolley).

Joe Lane became a legend of his own, embodying an Australian link to the bebop phenomenon. He was, Clare recounts, "in the habit of coming through the windows of musicians' rooms in the early hours with Charlie Parker records under his arm." Musicians who played and listened with Lane were caught up in the energy and the excitement of what Charlie Parker was doing. Seemingly a universe away from the context and the milieu in which this music was created, young musicians with a tendency to the new were fascinated and enthralled by its possibilities, and it was Joe Lane who was often responsible for opening the conceptual window as well as the occasional suburban one.[1]

These teenagers and young musicians are now an older generation. Their music, still strong, has become embedded in our own Australian section of the broader jazz landscape and they in turn are deeply important figures, innovators in their own time and context.

Joe (sometimes 'Killer') Lane was only two years younger than Charlie Parker and his link with that music was not just in his rare copies of Parker's recordings. Lane really understood it and was famous among musicians for his bebop phrasing. Describing him in a book about Bernie McGann in 1997, Geoff Page says that Lane was "an important connection between what younger players heard on records and what they actually played in the dance halls and other venues in Sydney and Melbourne."[2]

Sandy Evans says that when she was invited to write the music that would sit beside and under Yusef Komunyakaa's 14 sonnets, she had Lane's voice clearly in mind as one she wanted to write for. Knowing the links to Charlie Parker's music in the local scene made him an obvious choice. Obvious to Sandy, and obvious to those "in the know," but perhaps it's an inside story, little known outside the context of our own jazz history.

Others from that generation of musicians are Alan Turnbull (drums) and Chuck Yates (piano). Although compared to other local musicians, little has been written about them, these two are legends in the local scene, among the musicians they taught or worked with. They have been two of our busiest musicians, both touring extensively with big names from here and the United States. They both worked long stints at jazz clubs in Sydney and Melbourne, such as El Rocco, The Fat Black Pussy Cat and The Embers, which have since fallen away into legend, . Both Yates and Turnbull are low key about *Testimony* and about Bird's influence. Speaking to them separately, their tone is similar, a kind of "yes, of course, why do you need to ask?" "Charlie Parker had a huge influence," says Yates. "On all of us, and still does." It's obvious to him: no question.

Turnbull reminisces: he first heard Charlie Parker over the airwaves, via *Voice of America* in the 50s, along with other greats. It was a source of inspiration at the time, starting him on a journey that he's been on ever since. Asked about *Testimony,* he is full of admiration for what Evans achieved, particularly with her approach of having specific people in mind for particular parts of the suite. It's a response that turns out to be shared by many.

Both Yates and Turnbull have a level of experience that's almost impossible to achieve in today's Sydney or Melbourne . . . for one thing there simply isn't as much work now as there was, particularly in the seventies, eighties and nineties. They've also worked with many who are household names without becoming very well known themselves, outside some circles in the local jazz scene, making them strangely invisible to many audiences.

The writing, recording and performing of *Testimony* inevitably includes a number of inside stories—not just the anecdotes you'd expect from any production as large and complex as this one, but these types of hidden connections and significance that only reveal themselves with an exploration of the piece and those who played a part in bringing it to life.

Yet for *Testimony* to "work"—on radio, in a recording or on stage—it had to be able to be appreciated and hopefully enjoyed by an audience who might potentially have little to no exposure (much less understanding) of Charlie Parker's music, or of Yusef Komunyakaa's poetry and love of jazz, or of Sandy Evans or even the Australian jazz scene. It had to work for a general audience, as entertainment on a festival program. Even a toe in the water reveals that what lies behind the final *Testimony* is a complex, layered phenomenon. The surface of it—the performance as entertainment— stands alone, yet is greatly enriched by a little investigation.

Charlie Parker undoubtedly continues to make an impact, everywhere and here; cited for example as an important influence and inspiration by the likes of Bernie McGann, whose alto sound has been called one of the most distinctive and recognizable in the world today. Not only Bernie, but many others. Paul Cutlan (clarinet, bass clarinet, alto saxophone) remembers listening to the Massey Hall[3] recording lying in bed at age 14 and knowing it was something great. Sandy Evans reports excitement and exhilaration when she was first exposed to it. Hamish Stuart (drums) remembers seeing a transcription of some of Parker's music before he heard it and because of its complexity, at first glance thought it was classical music. These musicians are playing jazz in a context that requires no obligation to constantly look to the United States and to African American jazz musicians for inspiration, but Parker and his ilk continue to inspire. Mike Nock, based in Sydney, is another of Australia's links to an American style of jazz, via his extended time spent there and the connections he maintains today. He says of Charlie Parker's legacy and the relevance of it to an Australian idiom, that "the legacy of genius is that it does more than its creator could have imagined. It stretches further, rises higher, lasts longer. Genius extends beyond the milieu in which it was created."

But of course you would expect jazz musicians to know and have listened to the giants of their art form. *Testimony* does not rely on that knowledge and you do not need to be a musical insider to enjoy the recording. The work's foundation is the series of multiple testimonies to Parker, in multiple voices, through Yusef Komunyakaa's 14 sonnets. The poem makes *Testimony* what it is, yet the end result—on the recording or on stage—is greater than Komunyakaa's intrinsically beautiful and linguistically dense sonnets or their spare, fish-hooked narrative; greater than the textured sensuality of the music and greater than the breathtakingly clever staging and set. All are integral, and all contribute to the experience, in ways that simply would not have been possible anywhere else, whatever that might mean.

Musicians involved in *Testimony* count as "insiders," with their specialist musical knowledge that allows them inside the music and the narrative in ways not possible for a general audience. Yet as Clare asserts in *Bodgie Dada* "The truth is that many jazz musicians are not interested in words. . . . Music is the medium of the unsayable." Few musicians involved in the recording read Komunyakaa's poem before recording their pieces. In fact, asking them to recall their experience of *Testimony* ten years afterwards, the music itself is one of the three things they mention most. The other two "most memorable" aspects of the experience are consistently to do with Evans' tendency to push musicians to do their best, and her ability to unify musicians from disparate streams and idioms. Jackie Orszaczky (vocals and piccolo bass) and Lane (vocals) spring to mind as examples of this: the one with a name for funk, the other known as the father of bebop in Australia. These two, who have both sadly passed away since the recording of *Testimony,* were also singled out for special mention in Keith Gallasch's *Real Time Arts* review:

> some of the most eccentric moments were the most celebratory: Jackie Orszaczky singing and playing electric bass on Abel and Cain and the indefatigable Joe 'Bebop' Lane scatting on "Barrow Street" and "Moose the Mooch[e]."[4]

During recording, Evans provided a context for musicians at the beginning of their session, framing the piece they were about to record within the larger narrative and providing an affective context. Paul Cutlan remembers that this guidance gave him an idea of the emotional significance of a piece and then he was able to incorporate that into his playing during the session. Fitted together, individual sessions created this way succeeded in their emotional connection to the poetry.

Hamish Stuart, remarkably humble for a man of his abilities, remembers high anxiety during the recording of the song "Camarillo Part 2," which features vocals by Tanya Sparke. Asked about the impact of the text and the narrative of Komunyakaa's poem, he notes first that he was focusing on the music but then says that he remembers as he was reading the music and words, watching carefully for his cue, he felt completely taken over, saying "I was almost overwhelmed by what Tanya was singing." He remembers vividly the combined experience of being "blown away" and the sensation of dry-mouthed fear that he would mess something up. He didn't mess it up.

Tanya Sparke (vocals) first fell for jazz through the music of John Coltrane, Thelonius Monk, Charles Mingus and Billie Holiday. Not Holiday's words, though; not the narratives. She says it's the phrasing and time that attracted her—a musician's response to Lady Day. Sparke remembers *Testimony* was important for her individual practice as a musician. It provided validation of her outstanding singing abilities at a time when she needed it. "Camarillo Part 2" is set in the asylum that Charlie Parker ended up in. "I don't know about insanity, but I understood the stillness in this song," she says. "I was parenting three children at the time and that has its own psychological challenges." She related to the words she had to sing and rose to the emotional and physical challenge, although she maintains that this was possibly one of the easier pieces of music in the suite.

So yes, the music was a challenge and if it seems to feature here that's because it comes up again and again in musician reminiscences about *Testimony*. The experience for an audience may be broader but it is not surprising, ultimately, to hear that musicians have ears for the music.

The unifying experience of *Testimony* has also made a lasting impression on those involved. Hamish Stuart acknowledges that what Evans did may have been difficult with an earlier generation and simply impossible for a later one—if only because the passing of time inevitably leads to the loss of musicians to the scene. "Sandy is into bringing different colours to the palette," he says. "It may be that *Testimony* contributed to what we later saw happening more often—a kind of breaking down of stylistic and generational walls. Maybe it was just that laid-back Australian response that we took it all in our stride and downplayed it, but what happened was that people were working with others in ways that may not have been possible otherwise." *Testimony* for that reason alone has historical significance here.

Warwick Alder (trumpet) waxes lyrical about Evans' ability to stretch musicians when she gives them music to play. Others agree that she often seems to have a clearer idea of what a musician is capable of than musicians do themselves. Over the years she's been composing, arranging and playing, Evans has built a reputation of trustworthiness and the consensus seems to be that if she has faith in your musical ability, that faith is well-founded and you just need to get on with it and do your best. Plus a little bit extra.

Komunyakaa knew Evans too, at least by reputation, and is quoted in an interview at the time as saying, "[T]he bottom line was that Sandy was involved. I really trusted her expertise."[5]

Evans in turn, admits to being inspired by the power of Komunyakaa's words and says that the rhythmic and melodic structure of his text led naturally to the song forms she chose for each piece.[6]

Just as Charlie Parker's music is taught, played and appreciated around the world, Yusef Komunyakaa's poetry is known and loved well beyond the shores of the United States. His relationship with Sydney was more than that of a man "just passing through." He spent time in Australia, including a couple of extended stays of twelve months during the 1980s and was known to Chris Williams of our national broadcaster, the Australian Broadcasting Corporation (ABC), at least in part because he'd done some poetry readings for them during those stays. Komunyakaa's poem "February in Sydney" may be about other things, but it also exactly evokes oppressive, muggy, late summer Sydney with screaming clarity. "Blue Light Lounge Sutra for the Performance Poets at Harold Park

Hotel" is a well-known poem of Komunyakaa's exhorting the subject to push their art further, to:

> be ready
> to let the devil use your head
> for a drum

The Harold Park Hotel referred to in the title was an inner-city venue (recently revitalized) of such significance in the local jazz scene that when Jackie Orzcarsky passed away, his wake was held there. The links and resonances are sometimes accidental, but no less powerful for that. If this feels like a digression from the topic of *Testimony,* it is only partly so. These extra tidbits, discovered during exploration initiated by an interest in what lies beneath the surface of the work, reveal a hidden interplay between Charlie Parker and Sydney, facilitated by Komunyakaa—an interplay that extends beyond the poet's sonnets and the music that Sandy Evans created around them.

For the listener, the poem's narrative is arguably more present than it was for the musicians; it is certainly less interrupted. None of the musicians on the recording had a sense of the combined suite until well after the process was complete. The poem without the music has its own rhythms and a particular sinewy presence, made spare and yet dense by Komunyakaa's imagery. Striking, for an Australian listener trying to understand how such a powerful homage to a great American innovator comes to be presented in Sydney, is the imagery within the passage:

> Like a black cockatoo
> clinging to a stormy branch
> with its shiny head rocking
> between paradise & hell,
> that's how Yardbird
> listened.

There's no guarantee that more than a handful of us knew what a black cockatoo clinging to a stormy branch might look like, but its inclusion seems significant. It's an Australian image, or could be, which also goes for the eucalyptus elsewhere in the poem. And while the presence of eucalyptus trees in California is well known, and black cockatoos may exist on other continents, they are images that resonate strongly in the Australian breast. Wherever their reach may have extended since, this is where they came from.

Testimony was clearly a collaboration that went both ways, and not just in these hidden undercurrents of cockatoos and gum trees. In an interview in January 2002 with Philip McCarthy, Komunyakaa said of the scene:

> Australia takes its jazz very seriously, particularly in Sydney,
> and there are some very good players there. It wasn't the
> fact that they wanted to do it that was surprising, but that
> they had this very interesting creative vision about how they
> wanted to do it. [7]

But still, why here? Charlie Parker was an influence wherever jazz is played today. Was there something about an Australian sound that made this the right place? Opinions here vary about whether there is such a thing as an "Australian jazz" sound. It is to this question that the title of John Shand's 2009 book *Jazz: The Australian Accent* responds.[8] A recent favorite articulation of a possible response comes from Peter Kenneally, a local poet and jazz lover who reviewed a CD recently in sestina format:

> what is it that jazz sounds
> like in Australia? All the musings and jazzes of the world seem
> to seek asylum here, and after processing, we play with them.[9]

"and after processing, we play with them. . . ." Much as, I imagine, goes on in any place where jazz is being made and played.

Komunyakaa commented too, in that same 2002 interview:

Contemporary jazz is pretty international and I don't know that you can pick national origin from the sound any more. Sandy's work is an exceptional modern jazz composition and the national origin of the composer is not really relevant.[10]

So no, it probably wasn't the sound. But the creative vision was spectacular, the way the Australian Art Orchestra brought together Komunyakaa's poetry, Evans' composition, Nigel Jameison's staging. And maybe some combination of poet, composer, musicians and vision made this uniquely the right place for it. For those of us who were here, and were lucky enough to see *Testimony* performed, it certainly remains difficult to separate the words, music and creatively inspired set. Most reviews at the time discussed the staging, with its spectacular tiered structure, housing individual musicians in divided sections on three levels. Images were projected onto a large screen and singers performed on the stage in front. Inevitably this striking visual component became a focus. Surprisingly little was written about Komunyakaa's poetry at the time, but the music was reviewed widely by the local experts; people who know the scene and the musicians who play in it.

The layers and undercurrents—the stories beneath *Testimony*—will hopefully continue to reveal themselves over time. It played, after all, to an audience that included both the informed and uninformed. This was a festival gig at an Arts festival, not a jazz festival. There were probably people in the audience to whom Charlie Parker was a familiar name at best, who found out all they knew of him and his music by reading the program and listening to this concert. As for Komunyakaa's verses? Condense even the most mundane of lives into 14 sonnets and you're likely to miss some bits. Bird's life was not mundane, ergo bits have been missed. Not, thanks to the skill of the poet, to the detriment of the work.

What you hear on this recording is that Komunyakaa's and Evans' separate and combined gifts of capturing essence through image and sound have come together to create a moment of beauty. The unification of disparate elements has resulted in something larger and more important than perhaps anybody involved imagined.

Thanks to some unpredictably serendipitous connections, and a shared understanding by poet and composer of the way textures contribute to the telling of a story, we find ourselves connected in unimaginable ways to Charlie Parker and to the powerful languages of both poetry and jazz.

NOTES

1. Clare, John, and Gail Brennan. *Bodgie Dada & the Cult of Cool,* Sydney: UNSW Press, 1995.

2. Description of Joe Lane in Page, Geoff. *Bernie McGann, a life in Jazz.* NSW: Kardoorair Press, 1997.

3. *Jazz at Massey Hall,* 1953 recorded live at Massey Hall in Toronto, with "The Quintet"—Dizzy Gillespie, Charlie Parker, Bud Powell, Charles Mingus and Max Roach.

4. Keith Gallasch, "Sydney Festival: Myths, histories and projections," *Realtime Arts 47,* Feb-March 2002 realtimearts.net/article/47/6236.

5. Phillip McCarthy, "Review of *Testimony: The Legend of Charlie Parker,* Jazz Opera Poet Jams with the Bird," 9 January 2002 (aao.com.au /projects/review/testimony-the-legend-of-charlie-parker/4/).

6. Sandy Evans, "Composer's Notes," included in the Australian Art Orchestra program for *Testimony.*

7. Phillip McCarthy, "Review of *Testimony: The Legend of Charlie Parker,* Jazz Opera Poet Jams with the Bird."

8. John Shand, *Jazz: The Australian Accent,* UNSW Press, 2009.

9. Peter Kenneally, reviewing Paul Williamson's *In Cahoots* on the *Australian Jazz* website, AustralianJazz.net.

10. Phillip McCarthy, "Review of *Testimony: The Legend of Charlie Parker,* Jazz Opera Poet Jams with the Bird."

French Flowers Blooming

THE MUSIC FOR *TESTIMONY*

A discussion between Sandy Evans
& Christopher Williams

Having previously collaborated with Yusef Komunyakaa, Christopher Williams, a producer and director in Sydney, commissioned the poet to write a large-scale work for ABC Radio Drama in Australia. The following is an edited transcript from a production meeting between Christopher Williams and composer Sandy Evans in which they discuss creating the musical setting for Komunyakaa's libretto. It was first published in the Winter 1997 issue of *Brilliant Corners*.

Christopher Williams: What sounds do you hear in Yusef's poems?
Sandy Evans: The lines have a very strong musical quality. "Purple dress. Midnight-blue," for example, suggests to me rich chord colours and a similar mood to [the song] "Lover Man." The colours speak to me strongly in musical terms. Other lines indicate more rhythmic-based ideas. "He hopped boxcars to Chitown" suggests a kind of repetitive rhythm, probably more with spoken text. The lines "Bird was a pushover, a soft / touch for strings" point to a dichotomy between Western art, music, and jazz. And it's used metaphorically to talk about Parker's problems in his life as well.
Williams: So, you're looking for those kinds of clues?
Evans: Very much so. Partly because they are about music, so they give you strong musical indications, and also because of the nature of Yusef's writing, which has rhythmic cadences that suggest certain styles of music and moods and atmosphere. "Testimony" is a tribute to Charlie Parker, a celebration of his work and the tradition he comes out of, so I'm hoping, as a composer, to make my own tribute both to Parker and to all the other musicians who come up through the course of the text. I'm hoping to work with the inspirational qualities of those people, but also to find ways of using their musical language to interpret Yusef's text.

It's a very daunting task. There's a lot involved here. I could sit and read

105

the first section for an hour, and we're talking about interpreting that in maybe five minutes. Each section doesn't say one thing; it says hundreds and hundreds of things, and I think it's important that we present that complexity about Parker.

Williams: Yusef at one time proposed an alternative title, "Séance." How are we going to develop the sense of people keeping alive a memory or experience of Parker that actually conjures him into existence?

Evans: That's been the hardest question for me. I've been able to think of musicians that I would like to use for virtually every instrument other than the alto saxophone [laughs]. I mean, do you choose somebody who plays very closely to the style of Charlie Parker, or do you chose somebody who uses that as a staring point, but really is quite a different type of player?

My feeling at the moment is to find the alto player with a thorough understanding of bebop—who has connections to Parker and can move comfortably from there to a more contemporary style of playing. We're not trying to recreate Parker's band or Parker's life here. We're paying our own musical tribute to him, so we have to have respect for his work and the work of his contemporaries.

Williams: It's not merely a question of working on Charlie Parker's music but of allowing Charlie Parker's music to work on us.

Evans: Yeah. Very well put. I'm hoping to leave scope in the work for improvised input from most of the musicians, and possibly at times the singers, because I feel if we didn't do that then we would be losing the essential character of jazz.

Williams: There are many voices here and that's part of the principle of this work, and there is also tension between the single voice and the chorus. Some of the sections present more than one voice, and the chorus echoes the main line (and at times supplants it).

Evans: Yeah. Particularly in the section that begins "Moving eastward to the Deep / South" where we're talking about using a big band sound with the reference to Jay McShann, and having the male chorus there contrasted with the solo voice.

Then there's the connotation of slave music in "dragging balls & chains," and I think you'd suggested using that kind of phrase as a refrain for the male chorus. Where did we have it?

Williams: "For two days / he fingered a phantom alto / 'til 'What Price Love' spoke / through metal & fluted bone," and we got right into, "The band roared"—and that's obviously a useful cue.

Evans: Yeah, there's fantastic drama in that piece. I mean, it's all there in the text.

Williams: What kind of instrumentation do you hear there?

Evans: We're looking at twelve musicians, with traditional bebop instruments—piano, bass, drums, saxophone, trumpet—but trying to create a work that's definitely from a current perspective in terms of musical language, in terms of who I am as a composer. I'd like to use quite a lot of percussion: one percussionist with more of a background in Latin and African music, and the other more steeped in Western, classical traditions. I think the range of percussion is going to be an important factor to me in terms of the orchestration.

I'm not thinking of always having the whole bebop ensemble. I want to use violin, trombone, clarinet, some baritone sax. Blues guitar in the first section blends very well with the voice. I think that link with the blues is really important.

Williams: What do you think you'd like the audience to take away from an experience of this work?

Evans: Well, I don't know if there's a simple answer to that. I'd like them not to have been confused. I think music in itself is complex—and as soon as you ask people to grasp other things it's easy to confuse them, you know? Most people who will listen to it will have certain preconceptions about what the piece is about and, though it may sound a bit corny, I want to take them on a journey.

Williams: Going where?

Evans: Experiencing the qualities that Parker's music has had on me: beauty; excitement and intensity; virtuosity. I think there is tension in it. I think the historical reference, while still being contemporary, is important. And the normal things you would hope for in a composition: that it doesn't get boring; that it makes sense. But the overriding things to me are the passionate intensity, stunning virtuosity, and the beauty of the music.

Williams: I'd like to leave the audience with a clear sense of the ways in which Parker affected people; why he's become an important figure; what kind of impact he's had on people's lives on an individual level and how that's added up to an influence on a cultural level. Often you say of geniuses that they stand on giants' shoulders. Well, I don't know that there was *a* giant's shoulders on which Charlie Parker stood. He rode on the collective shoulders of a whole people, in both their social and musical aspects. So it's important to show that connection. To pay respect. To pay him his due in terms of his achievement of the beauty and the other qualities you've identified, musically. And, to take the séance idea more literally, to conjure the spirit of Charlie Parker by remembering him, paying testimony to him.

There's a spiritual and religious component, too, that I think is essential as a kind of unifying idea. That's not to, you know, make a saint or canonize him—

Evans: No—

Williams: —but to recognize him as a mythical figure, over and above the historical person. He was not a super-human character, and that makes his achievements all the more remarkable.

Evans: I think the pain of his life is something we have to really deal with, too.

Williams: Yeah, well, there's a parallel between the life of a saint and the representation of Parker here, where you've got the character who's fairly wayward and has a revelation—

Evans: When he could finally play on "Cherokee"?

Williams: Yeah. There's that moment of apotheosis. It's a revelation, and he sees the way ahead of him, despite wrestling with so many demons. There are parallels, which I find fascinating between a traditional life of a saint from the Early Christian Church and Parker's journey through his musical and personal life, which lends him a mythic status.

You can read in the last section where a soldier of a supposedly enemy nation has this Charlie Parker recording in his hand and he clutches that in his dying moments. Then there are the sightings of Parker in the Buddha, in the Sphinx, which is analogous with the sightings of saints after their deaths. So I think there's a wonderful kind of beatification in the writing.

Evans: A lot of religious knowledge is also transferred from teacher to disciple, and, musically speaking, that's very much the case with Charlie Parker. Virtually anybody anywhere in the world who takes up the saxophone hears his teacher tell him to go listen to Charlie Parker. Parker's spirit and his knowledge are guiding principles for so many people in so many different places.

Composer/Musical Director's Notes
Sandy Evans

> All the players we look up to historically have learned in a
> social context by listening to other players, whether on CD or
> actually going out and playing with them.[1]

I can still remember the exhilaration I felt on first hearing a recording of
Charlie Parker. The energy, virtuosity, passion, innovation, spontaneity,
intelligence and sheer beauty of his playing remain to this day an artistic
pinnacle that I will never come close to reaching, but for which I am
constantly striving.

In 1995, Christopher Williams invited me to collaborate with Yusef
Komunyakaa on a music-theatre project for radio with jazz as its central
language. Christopher was a radio drama producer with the Australian
Broadcasting Corporation (ABC). The ABC commissioned *Testimony*
with assistance from the Music Board of the Australia Council. Thanks
to Roz Cheney, then arts editor at ABC Radio National, for her support.
Testimony was first broadcast on Soundstage, ABC Classic FM in August
1999. The ABC recording, made under my musical direction and produced
by Christopher Williams, is included in this publication.

In writing the music for *Testimony* I was challenged and inspired not
only by the life and music of Bird and his contemporaries, but also by the
extraordinary way Yusef told Bird's story. The emotive power of his words,
and the rhythmic and melodic flow of each sonnet led naturally to the
song forms and singers I chose for each composition. The singers showcase
the diversity and excellence of vocal talent in Sydney in the late 1990s;
strong, individual voices who were integral to my creative vision. The
musicians on this recording are a who's who of the Sydney jazz scene at
that time. I am honored to have worked with these great artists who are
at the heart of the Australian jazz culture I love.

I am proud to present the exquisite cast of vocalists featured in

Testimony. The unique voice and musical personality of each one was my bridge between Yusef's poetry and the musical framework of the compositions. Without exception, the vocalists took my score and made music that was beautiful beyond my wildest dreams. I remember coming home from rehearsals and recording sessions blown away by the depth of emotion and nuance they brought to my melodies. Of course they were responding first and foremost to Yusef's words and Parker's story, but to be part of this triumvirate as a composer was an extraordinary privilege. Several poems worked best in spoken form and are beautifully narrated by Michael Edward-Stevens.

This recording is graced by two American jazz legends, Kurt Elling and Laurence Hobgood, who joined Sydney musicians Jonathan Zwartz and Hamish Stuart to bring their superb artistry and wit to "A Day Like Today."

Testimony is also 'testimony' to two legendary figures in Australian music, Joe 'Bebop' Lane and Jackie Orszaczky who, sadly, have both passed away since this recording was made.

Joe Lane was one of a handful of early bebop pioneers in Australia. His passion for Charlie Parker's music continued throughout his entire life. He spent his last years in a nursing home in Sydney, unable to speak as the result of a stroke. Miraculously, Joe was still able to sing Charlie Parker solos, even though he couldn't even say hello to hospital staff or visitors. His good friend and contemporary Chuck Yates (piano), visited him in hospital often during these years, and together they brought Parker's legacy to life in a particularly poignant musical dialogue far removed from Parker's home in time and place, but very close in spirit.

Jackie Orszaczky was a Hungarian born Australian deeply loved for his soulful groove, keen musical insight, incisive wit, warmth and humanity. Nobody in Australia embodied the feeling at the heart of blues, soul, funk, jazz and R&B as deeply as Jackie. His life partner, Tina Harrod joins him on the track "Abel and Cain" where their voices resonate in glorious union, as they often did at live gigs, holding the audience enraptured between ecstasy, pain and the overwhelming desire to get up and dance. Thankfully Tina's passionate performances are one of the mainstays of the current Australian music scene. Two musicians who were incredibly important in the development and recording of *Testimony,* drummer Hamish Stuart and trombonist James Greening, were among Jackie's closest friends and musical associates.

Chuck Yates, Bernie McGann (alto saxophones) and Alan Turnbull (drums) are highly esteemed veterans of the bebop and post-bop scene in Australia. Their appearances on this recording are very special to me. They belong to a small handful of jazz innovators in Australia who have dedicated their lives to performing this great music, arguably at times with a particularly Australian aesthetic. They have influenced generations of younger players, many of whom appear on this recording. Bass players Lloyd Swanton and Jonathan Zwartz, and trumpet player Warwick Alder, have been long-term members of Bernie McGann's small groups. James Greening (trombone) and myself have also performed extensively with Bernie, both as members of John Pocheé's large ensemble, Ten Part Invention (of which Warwick is also a member) and as guests with Bernie's trio.

The stories surrounding each of the musicians on this recording are worthy of much greater attention than I am giving them here. None of these musicians wear style as an accouterment. Each of them lives their music deeply: the blues of Tina Harrod, Dave Brewer and Lachlan Doley; the harmonic, textural and rhythmic sophistication of Lily Dior, Kristen Cornwell, Alister Spence and Jeremy Sawkins; the woodwind artistry of Paul Cutlan and Casey Greene, the lead trumpet of Bob Coassin; the Latin heat of Toni Allayialis and Fabian Hevia; the swinging elegance of Kate Swadling and Pamela Knowles; the 'loveknots and chords' of Michele Morgan, John Rodgers, Steve Elphick and Simon Barker; and the aching beauty of Tanya Sparke.

On a personal note, the day the ABC funding of *Testimony* was confirmed was the same day my husband, Tony Gorman, music producer of *Testimony* was diagnosed with multiple sclerosis. At that time, Tony was primarily a jazz alto saxophonist. We had worked together extensively in the previous decade, especially with pianist Alister Spence in the group Clarion Fracture Zone. Lloyd Swanton and Steve Elphick were members of that group.

Simon Barker and Hamish Stuart also appeared with the band as guest performers. As I wrote the music for *Testimony,* I lived through the painful experience of watching my husband, a passionate alto saxophonist, lose his ability to do what he most loved. This may seem irrelevant to the central story of *Testimony,* but this highly personal experience collided with Parker's story and Yusef's poetry in my creative process, and it had an important influence on the music I wrote.

I am indebted to Christopher Williams for his inspiration, guidance and dedication in the development and recording of this work. The masterful soundscape that frames this aural journey was created by the skillful ears of engineers Russell Stapleton, Stephen Tilley and music producer Tony Gorman.

I was delighted when the Australian Art Orchestra (AAO), an ensemble overflowing with brilliant soloists and original thinkers, decided to perform *Testimony* live. The evolution from radio show to live performance was thrilling. AAO artistic director Paul Grabowsky invited eminent director Nigel Jamieson to stage the live performance. Nigel assembled a brilliant creative team whose spectacular staging of *Testimony* in the Concert Hall at the Sydney Opera House was a highlight of the Sydney Festival in 2002, and of my career. Special thanks to Wendy Martin and Ann Moir for their crucial roles in this production.

It is a composer's dream to have the kind of support I received in the recording and performance of *Testimony*. Sincere thanks to all those whose talent and commitment made this a reality.

I have had the privilege of living with Yusef's words for a long time. They are part of me now, yet they still shock me with their unexpected revelations and cutting emotions. Thank you Yusef for trusting me to create music to live with them.

NOTE

1. "Sandy Evans in Conversation with Michael Webb," *Extempore* 1:1, November 2008, 23–39.

Testimony, Songs and Musicians
Sandy Evans

I orchestrated each of Yusef's poems in response to the affective emotion and aesthetics of the narrative. A unique band was formed for every composition, each one featuring vocalists and musicians who embodied particular expressive qualities intrinsic in the text.

TESTIMONY OVERTURE

"Moose the Mooche," "Relaxin' at Camarillo," "Dewey Square,"
    Charlie Parker; "52nd Street Theme," Thelonious Monk.

Bernie McGann (alto saxophone)

Sandy Evans (tenor saxophone)

Casey Greene (baritone saxophone, flute)

Paul Cutlan (bass clarinet)

Warwick Alder (trumpet)

Bob Coassin (trumpet)

James Greening (trombone)

John Rodgers (violin)

Alister Spence (piano, keyboards)

Lloyd Swanton (bass)

Hamish Stuart (drums)

BOXCARS

Michael Edward-Stevens (spoken words)

Paul Cutlan (alto sax, clarinet, bass clarinet)

Sandy Evans (tenor saxophone)

Casey Greene (flute)

Warwick Alder (trumpet)

Alister Spence (keyboards)

Dave Brewer (guitar)

Lloyd Swanton (bass)

Hamish Stuart (drums)

CHICKEN SHACK PART 1
Music: "If I Had You," Irving Berlin.
Michael Edward-Stevens (spoken words)
Chuck Yates (piano)

CHICKEN SHACK PART 2
Music: "Ko Ko," Charlie Parker.
Michael Edward-Stevens (spoken words)
Bernie McGann (alto saxophone)
Warwick Alder (trumpet)
Chuck Yates (piano)
Jonathan Zwartz (bass)
Alan Turnbull (drums)

PURPLE DRESS
Kristen Cornwell (vocals)
Sandy Evans (tenor saxophone)
Jeremy Sawkins (guitar)
Jonathan Zwartz (bass)
Hamish Stuart (drums)

DEEP SOUTH
Kate Swadling (vocals)
Paul Cutlan (alto saxophone [alto solo], bass clarinet, clarinet)
Bernie McGann (alto saxophone)
Sandy Evans (tenor saxophone)
Casey Greene (baritone saxophone)
Bob Coassin (trumpet)
James Greening (trombone)
Alister Spence (trombone)
Lloyd Swanton (bass)
Hamish Stuart (drums)

A DAY LIKE TODAY

Kurt Elling (vocals)

Laurence Hobgood (piano)

Jonathan Zwartz (bass)

Hamish Stuart (drums)

ABEL AND CAIN

Jackie Orszaczky (vocals)

Tina Harrod (vocals)

Dave Brewer (guitar)

Jackie Orszaczky (piccolo bass)

Lloyd Swanton (bass)

Hamish Stuart (percussion)

BLACK COCKATOO

Toni Allayialis (vocals)

Paul Cutlan (alto saxophone, [alto solo])

Sandy Evans (tenor saxophone)

Casey Greene (baritone saxophone, flute)

Bob Coassin (trumpet)

Warwick Alder (trumpet)

James Greening (trombone)

Alister Spence (piano)

Lloyd Swanton (bass)

Fabian Hevia (drums, percussion)

CAMARILLO PART 1

Michael Edward-Stevens (spoken words)

Sandy Evans (soprano saxophone)

Paul Cutlan (bass clarinet, clarinet)

John Rodgers (violin)

Alister Spence (piano)

Hamish Stuart (drums)

CAMARILLO PART 2
Tanya Sparke (vocals)
Paul Cutlan (alto saxophone)
Sandy Evans (tenor saxophone)
Alister Spence (piano)
Lloyd Swanton (bass)
Hamish Stuart (drums)

ADDIE'S BOY
Pamela Knowles (vocals)
Bernie McGann (alto saxophone)
Chuck Yates (piano)
Jonathan Zwartz (bass)
Alan Turnbull (drums)

PREE'S FUNERAL SONG
Michael Edward-Stevens (spoken words)
Tina Harrod (vocals)
James Greening (trombone, pocket trumpet)
Lachlan Doley (organ)
Jonathan Zwartz (bass)
Hamish Stuart (drums)

BARROW STREET
Joe "Bebop" Lane (vocals)
Jonathan Zwartz (bass)

MOOSE THE MOOCHE
Charlie Parker.
Joe "Bebop" Lane (vocals)
Bernie McGann (alto saxophone)
Warwick Alder (trumpet)
Chuck Yates (piano)
Jonathan Zwartz (bass)
Alan Turnbull (drums)

A SOFT TOUCH FOR STRINGS

Michele Morgan (vocals)

John Rodgers (violin)

Steve Elphick (bass)

Simon Barker (drums)

BARONESS PANNONICA

Lily Dior (vocals)

John Rodgers (violin)

Bernie McGann (alto saxophone)

Sandy Evans (tenor saxophone)

Paul Cutlan (bass clarinet)

Warwick Alder (trumpet)

James Greening (trombone)

Alister Spence (piano)

Lloyd Swanton (bass)

Hamish Stuart (drums)

TESTIMONY FINALE

Based on "Dewey Square," Charlie Parker.

Michael Edward-Stevens (spoken words)

Sandy Evans (tenor saxophone, soprano saxophone, flute)

Warwick Alder (trumpet)

James Greening (bass trombone)

Alister Spence (piano)

Jonathan Zwartz (bass)

Hamish Stuart (drums)

TESTIMONY CODA

Lily Dior (vocals)

Bernie McGann (alto saxophone)

Chuck Yates (piano)

Australian Art Orchestra Performances
Paul Grabowsky

Charlie Parker's contribution to the art and culture of the twentieth century must be compared to that of Stravinsky, Picasso or Joyce. A protean modernist, his improvisations encrypt the entire known Western musical syntax of his time into a language in which the commonplace is elevated to the same status as the arcane, the whimsical plays freely with the mordant, in which the bar line disappears, literally blown out of the way by a force which lives only as pulse, the same clock that drives life itself. Imitated by many, rivaled by few, his colossal domination of the bebop form becomes clear when that form is compared to what succeeded it, namely the classicizing structures of hard bop, in which the freedom of Bird's legacy was replaced by paradigms of harmonic, rhythmic and melodic behavior. Not until Ornette Coleman's toy horn blew into the Half Note club in 1959 would jazz feel the hot wind of freedom again.

It is in recognizing this freedom, which lies at the heart of jazz, we come again and again to Parker's legacy. The philosophy that underlies the AAO is one that recognizes the validity of the spontaneous utterance as the essential creative moment in art, arising out of an artist's personal agony with the materials and influences which form the artistic person-ality. Parker was able to give form and eloquence to this moment like no other, his soaring melodies the result of infinite computations and deci-sions made at the speed of thought, performed on instruments much more awkward to play than the balanced-action saxophones of today, horns often held together with rubber bands and chewing gum.

Dead at 34, Parker took on the status of redeemer and sacrificial lamb in a milieu which claimed the lives of many way too soon: Bix Beider-becke, Fats Navarro, Clifford Brown, Booker Little, even John Coltrane. Bird's tragedy is unveiled subtly and sweetly in Yusef Komunyakaa's verses, and set gorgeously, wittily and wisely by Sandy Evans. As inheritors in some way of Parker's bequest, each of us has a personal tribute to pay, and within the structures of Sandy's scores is the space to allow for those personal testimonials to occur. We wanted to create a space of reflection, a ritual, a theatre in which this process can be shared, hence we invited our friends Nigel Jamieson and Dan Potra to help us realize this tribute.

Premiére: 16 January 2002, Concert Hall,
   Sydney Opera House, Sydney Festival

TOUR HISTORY
   2002—Concert Hall, Sydney Opera House, Sydney Festival
   2002—Melbourne Concert Hall, Melbourne International
      Arts Festival
   2003—Festival Theatre, Adelaide Cabaret Festival

Composer: Sandy Evans
Libretto: Yusef Komunyakaa
Theatre Director: Nigel Jamieson
Musical Directors: Sandy Evans, Paul Grabowsky
Set Design: Dan Porta
Image Design: Andrew Savage
Sound Design: John O'Donnell
Lighting Design: John Rayment
Original Commission: Christopher Williams, ABC Audio Arts, 1995
Producer: Wendy Martin

PERFORMERS
Vocalists: Toni Allayialis, Dan Barnett, Kristen Cornwell, Lily
   Dior, Tina Harrod, Joe 'Bebop' Lane, Michele Morgan, Jackie
   Orszaczky, Shelley Scown, Tanya Sparke, Kate Swadling
Narrator: Bobby C (Sydney), Ajaye (Melbourne and Adelaide)
AAO Musicians: Sandy Evans, (reeds); Lachlan Davidson, (reeds);
   Paul Cutlan, (reeds); Julien Wilson, (reeds); Elliott Dalgleish,

(reeds); Bob Coassin, (trumpet); Scott Tinkler, (trumpet); Phillip Slater, (trumpet); James Greening, (trombone); Adrian Sherriff, (bass trombone); Philip Rex, (tuba /double bass); John Rodgers, (violin); Carl Dewhurst, (guitar); Paul Grabowsky, (piano); Alister Spence, (piano and keyboards); Gary Costello, (double bass); Niko Schauble, (drums); Alex Pertout, (percussion); Vanessa Tomlinson, (percussion).

YUSEF KOMUNYAKAA, professor and Senior Distinguished Poet at New York University's Graduate Creative Writing Program, has authored eighteen books of poetry and fourteen performance works in addition to poetry, prose and plays collected in numerous anthologies and journals in the United States and abroad. His many awards include the Wallace Stevens Award in 2011 and the Robert Creeley Award in 2007. He was elected to the American Academy of Arts and Letters in 2009 and won the Pulitzer Prize for Poetry in 1994.

RACHEL ELIZA GRIFFITHS

Komunyakaa describes his birthplace, Bogalusa, Louisiana, as "terror and beauty living side by side"—a foundational tension he would build his life's work upon, and a theme he ultimately captures in "Testimony," his tribute to Charlie Parker. Komunyakaa's work, education and curiosity have prompted travel and relocation across the United States and the world. It was during his second Australian sabbatical that Christopher Williams approached him with the idea of writing the libretto for Williams' radio-performance brainchild, *Testimony.*

Before attending university, Yusef served in the United States Army as an information specialist during the Vietnam War. He received the Bronze Star for his journalistic work with the *Southern Cross.*

Rocky Mountain Creative Arts Journal published his first book of poems, *Dedications and Other Dark Horses,* in 1977. He followed with *Lost in the Bonewheel Factory* in 1979. In 1984, Yusef Komunyakaa received widespread recognition for *Copacetic,* which through rhythm and language embraces a tangible jazz influence. He followed *Copacetic* with *Toys in a Field,* a chapbook (1986); *I Apologize for the Eyes in My Head* (1986), winner of the San Francisco Poetry Center Award; and *Dien Cai Dau* (1988), which won the Dark Room Poetry Prize.

Since then, he has published several books of poems, including *Warhorses* (2008); *Gilgamesh* (2006), a drama in verse; *Taboo: The Wishbone Trilogy, Book 1* (2004); *Pleasure Dome: New & Collected Poems, 1975–1999* (2001); *Talking Dirty to the Gods* (2000); *Thieves of Paradise* (1998), a finalist for the National Book Critics Circle Award; *Neon Vernacular: New and Selected Poems, 1977–1989* (1994), for which he received the Pulitzer Prize, the Kingsley Tufts Poetry Award and the William Faulkner Award; *Magic City* (1992) and *February in Sydney*, a chapbook (1989). His most recent collection, *The Chameleon Couch* (2011), was nominated for the National Book Award and the National Book Critics Circle Award.

Yusef Komunyakaa's prose is collected in *Condition Red: Essays, Interviews, and Commentaries,* edited by Radiclani Clytus (forthcoming); *Conversations with Yusef Komunyakaa,* edited by Shirley A. James Hanshaw (2010); and *Blue Notes: Essays, Interviews & Commentaries* edited by Radiclani Clytus (2000). He also co-edited *The Jazz Poetry Anthology* (1991) and *The Second Set: The Jazz Poetry Anthology Volume 2* (1996) with Sascha Feinstein.

SANDY EVANS, an Australian saxophonist and composer living in Sydney, has a passion for improvisation and the creation of new music. She has composed a significant body of works for her performance groups— the Sandy Evans Trio and Sextet, The Australian Art Orchestra, MARA!, Clarion Fracture Zone, GEST8, Ten Part Invention, The catholics, austraLYSIS, Waratah—and many Australian jazz, intercultural and new music ensembles.

Sandy's keen interest in Indian jazz collaboration led her to undertake doctoral research at Macquarie University. She performs with South Indian mridangam maestro Guru Kaaraikkudi Mani, as well as Sydney based musicians Sarangan Sriranganathan and Bobby Singh.

Her numerous awards include the inaugural Bell Award for Australian

Jazz Musician Of The Year 2003; a Young Australian Creative Fellowship; the APRA Award; two Mo Awards; and three ARIA Awards. In 2010, Sandy was awarded an Order of Australia Medal (OAM) at the Queen's Birthday Honours for services to the arts.

Sandy tours extensively in Australia, Europe, Canada and Asia. She appears in the Australian jazz documentaries *Beyond El Rocco* and *Dr Jazz,* and has been featured in over thirty albums. In 2001, Evans inaugurated a jazz improvisation course for young women, which the Sydney Improvised Music Association (SIMA) runs annually. She teaches and tutors at the university and grammar school levels, runs saxophone workshops and participates in "Music Viva In Schools" programs throughout Australia. For information on Sandy's current projects and her remarkable work, please visit her website, sandyevans.com.au.

SASCHA FEINSTEIN received the 2008 Pennsylvania's Governor's Award for Artist of the Year. He is the author of two poetry collections: *Ajanta's Ledge* and *Misterioso* (winner of the Hayden Carruth Award). His other books include a memoir, *Black Pearls: Improvisations on a Lost Year;* a collection of interviews, *Ask Me Now: Conversations on Jazz & Literature;* and a critical study, *Jazz Poetry: From the 1920s to the Present.* He has also co-edited four books: *The Jazz Poetry Anthology* and its companion volume *The Second Set*

(both with Yusef Komunyakaa), *The Jazz Fiction Anthology* (with David Rife), and *Keystone Korner: Portrait of a Jazz Club* (with Kathy Sloane).

A frequent contributor to *JAZZIZ* magazine, he has published work in *American Poetry Review, The Southern Review, African American Review, The Wallace Stevens Journal, The Penguin Book of the Sonnet, The New Grove Dictionary of Jazz,* and elsewhere. In 1996, he founded *Brilliant Corners: A Journal of Jazz & Literature,* which he still edits. He teaches at Lycoming College and in the MFA in writing program at Vermont College of Fine Arts. For more information about Sascha Feinstein and *Brilliant Corners,* please visit Sascha's website, Sascha.Feinstein.com.

CHRISTOPHER WILLIAMS is a director/producer, dramaturg and sound artist—working with radiophonic and acousmatic composition, soundscape, sound installation, and electro-acoustic music. He has produced over one hundred radiophonic works for ABC Radio National, Classic FM and Online. He has directed over twenty theatre productions across Australia. Christo-

pher's electronic studio project is *The Strange Mechanism,* and he performs with his electro-acoustic ensemble *Revolution 9.*

In 1995, Christopher commissioned Yusef Komunyakaa and Sandy Evans to write and compose *Testimony,* a tribute to the life and music of Charlie Parker. His production was first broadcast by the Australian Broadcasting Corporation in 1999.

He studied Contemporary Improvised Music at the University of Sydney; Drama at the University of New South Wales; and trained in Directing at National Institute of Dramatic Art (NIDA), the Australian Opera, and at the Australian Film, Television and Radio School (AFTRS). He is currently undertaking a PhD in Contemporary Radiophonic Dramaturgy, Composition and Production at the University of Technology, Sydney.

Christopher has been internationally recognised with the Prix Italia for Radio Drama (1998); a Special Commendation for Sound Design at the

Prix Italia (2007), and a medal at the 2006 New York Festival. His work has been nominated for the Prix Italia (1998, 2000, 2004, 2007, 2010); the Prix Marulic (2003, 2005), and the Karl Sczuka Preis (2000). In 1997 in Ravenna, he was made President of the Radio Drama Jury of the Prix Italia.

Career highlights include the composition, direction and design of his quadraphonic contemporary music-theatre work *As if Electrically Controlled* at IHOS Opera, Hobart; creating sound for the installation *Uneasily Along the Sand* at the Mildura Palimpsest Festival; exhibiting *Four Works for Headphones* at the Dianne Tanzer Gallery, Melbourne and the Horsham and Swan Hill Regional Art Galleries; performing at *Earpoke* for the Australasian Computer Music Conference and at COMA with *Revolution 9;* and performing with Nicholas Collins at RIA in *Works of Slightly Misused Technology;* directing the première production of *Low* by Daniel Keene at Sydney's Belvoir St Theatre; and co-producing international radiophonic productions with West Deutscher Rundfunk (*Crashing Aeroplanes*) with Andreas Ammer and FM Einheit) and Bayerischer Rundfunk (*Vanishing Points* with Klaus Buhlert).

MIRIAM ZOLIN is based in Melbourne, Australia and is an enthusiastic supporter of jazz. As the publisher and managing editor at *Extempore* and *Australian Jazz* she is also responsible for publishing poetry, fiction, interviews, features and essays with a special emphasis on writing inspired by jazz and improvised music. Her novel *Tristessa & Lucido* (UQP, 2003) and her current work in progress *Releasing Artful* both have jazz themes. She also writes on other subjects and her non-fiction has appeared in *Australian Book Review; Griffith Review; Cordite Poetry Review; The Canberra Times* and the *Sydney Morning Herald.* Her short stories have appeared in *Sleepers*

CHAMINDA SUBASINGHE

Almanac No 7; the UTS writer's anthology, *Small Suburban Crimes;* and the University of Melbourne graduate literary collection, *Muse.* Please visit *Australian Jazz,* australianjazz.net and *Extempore,* extempore.com.au or Miriam's blog, miriamzolin.com.

PAUL GRABOWSKY, pianist, composer, arranger and conductor, is one of Australia's most respected artists. He has written the scores for over twenty feature films in Australia, the United Kingdom and United States including *The Eye of the Storm* and *Last Orders* (Fred Schepisi); *Innocence* (Paul Cox); and *Shiner* (John Irvin). Among the many other filmmakers he has worked with are Gillian Armstrong, Nadia Tass and Clara Law. His television credits include the series *Phoenix and Janus* and the Emmy-winning *Empire Falls.* His works for the theatre include two operas and various multimedia works.

Paul is the founder and Artistic Director of the Australian Art Orchestra, with which he tours both nationally and internationally. Among his numerous CD releases are two for the *Hush* series (for which he is Artistic Director), designed to assist in the healing environment of Melbourne Children's Hospital. He has won four ARIA awards, two Helpmann awards, several Bell Awards and a Deadly award. He was the Sydney Myer Performing Artist of the Year in 2000, and received the Melbourne Prize for Music in 2007. For updates, please visit The Australian Art Orchestra's website, aao.com.au or Paul Grabowsky's personal site: paulgrabowsky.com.

Testimony Australian Art Orchestra Performance Reviews

Philip McCarthy, "Jazz Opera Poet Jams With the Bird," Australian Art
Orchestra, aao.com.au/ignore/reviews-performance/post/-jazz-opera
-poet-jams-with-the-bird/ 9 January 2002.
Lynden Barber, "Swinging in Bird's Paradise," *The Australian,* 11 January
2002.
Keith Gallasch, "Excellent," *Real Time,* January 2002.
Hilary Schrubb, "Soaring Tribute to Jazzman Bird," *The Australian,* 18
January 2002.
John Shand, "A True Marriage of Sound and Vision Sees Bird Take
Flight," *Sydney Morning Herald,* 18 January 2002.
Patrick McDonald, "Tribute to a Genius," *The Advertiser,* 10 June 2003.

Yusef Komunyakaa

The Chameleon Couch, Farrar, Straus and Giroux, 2011.
Warhorses, Farrar Strauss and Giroux, 2008.
Gilgamesh, Wesleyan University Press, 2006.
Taboo, Farrar Straus Giraux, 2004.
Pleasure Dome: New and Collected Poems, Wesleyan University Press,
2001.
Blue Notes: Essays, Interviews, and Commentaries, edited by Radiclani
Clytus, University of Michigan Press, 2000.
Talking Dirty to the Gods, Farrar, Straus, 2000.
Thieves of Paradise, Wesleyan University Press, 1998.
(Editor with Sascha Feinstein) *The Second Set: The Jazz Poetry Anthology,
Volume 2,* Indiana University Press, 1996.
Neon Vernacular: New and Selected Poems, Wesleyan University Press,
1993.

Magic City, Wesleyan University Press/University Press of New England, 1992.

(Editor with Sascha Feinstein) *The Jazz Poetry Anthology,* Indiana University Press, 1991.

February in Sydney (chapbook), Matchbooks, 1989.

Dien Cai Dau, Wesleyan University Press, 1988.

Toys in a Field, Black River Press, 1986.

I Apologize for the Eyes in My Head, Wesleyan University Press, 1986.

Copacetic, Wesleyan University Press, 1984.

Lost in the Bonewheel Factory, Lynx House Press, 1979.

Dedications and Other Darkhorses, RMCAJ, 1977.

SELECTED DISCOGRAPHY

Sandy Evans

With Guru Kaaraikkudi Mani and Sruthi Laya
  Cosmic Waves (Underscore Records) 2012.

MARA!
  Tra Parole E Silenzio with the Martenitsa Choir (Mara Music) 2012.
  Sezoni with the Martenitsa Choir (Real World) 1997.
  Ruino Vino (Rufus) 1995.
  Don't Even Think (Sandstock) 1990.

Sandy Evans Sextet
  When the Sky Cries Rainbows (SET) 2011.

SNAP
  Boggy Creek Bop (Rufus) 2010.

Sandy Evans Trio
  The Edge of Pleasure (SET) 2009.
  Not in the Mood (Newmarket) 2002.

The catholics
  Inter Vivos - Live in Concert (Bugle) 2009.
  Village (Bugle)2007.
  Gondola (Bugle) 2006.
  Choice, (Bugle) 2000.
  Barefoot (Bugle) 1999.
  Life On Earth (Rufus) 1997.
  Simple (Rufus) 1994.
  The Catholics (Rufus) 1992.

GEST8
  Kaleidoscope (Tall Poppies) 2008.

The Australian Art Orchestra

The Chennai Sessions (AAO) 2008.

Ruby (AAO) 2005.

The Theft of Sita (Newmarket) 2000.

Into The Fire (AAO) 1999.

Passion (ABC) 1999.

Kim Sanders and Friends

Bent Grooves (MMKS) 2007.

Ten Part Invention

Live at Wangaratta (ABC) 2005.

Unidentified Spaces (Rufus) 2000.

Tall Stories (Rufus) 1994.

Clarion Fracture Zone

Canticle with the Martenitsa Choir (Rufus) 2002.

Less Stable Elements (Rufus) 1996.

What This Love Can Do (Rufus) 1994.

Zones on Parade (Rufus) 1993.

Blue Shift (Rufus) 1990-1991.

The Gai Bryant Quartet

Music (GB) 2002.

High Jinx (Rufus) 1998.

Paul McNamara

Duo Logic (Rufus) 1999.

austraLYSIS

Present Tense (Tall Poppies) 1997.

The Next Room (Tall Poppies) 1994.

Moving the Landscapes (Tall Poppies) 1992.

The Bernie McGann Trio

Playground (Rufus) 1997.

Jeremy Sawkins
   Toys (Rufus Records) 1994.

Judy Bailey and Friends
   Sundial (ABC) 1993.

Jamie Fielding
   Notes From The Underground (Australian Independent
   Jazz Artists) 1983.

Yusef Komunyakaa

With Tomas Doncker and The Shape Shifter Ensemble, *The Mercy
   Suite* (Future Roots Music) 2008.
With Dennis Gonzalez, *Herido Live at St. James Cathedral, Chicago*
   (8th Harmonic Breakdown, Inc.) 2001.
*Our Souls Run Deep Like the Rivers, Notable recordings of African
   American Poets,* "Facing It" and "Venus's Flytrap" (Rhino) 2000.
With vocalist Pamela Knowles, *Thirteen Kinds of Desire* (Pamela
   Knowles) 2000.
Yusef Komunyakaa and Sharon Olds (The Academy of American Poets
   Audio Archive) 1999.
With John Tchicai jazz ensemble, *Love Notes from the Madhouse,*
   poems from *New Vernacular* and *Thieves of Paradise* (8th Harmonic
   Breakdown, Inc.) 1998.
Yusef Komunyakaa (San Francisco Poetry Center) 1998.
With Elliot Goldenthal, *Fire Water Paper: A Vietnam Oratorio,* "You
   and I are Disappearing," and "Boat People" (Sony Classical) 1996.

ACKNOWLEDGMENTS

Thanks, Sandy and Christopher. I'm still surprised by how the spirit
of Charlie Parker worked on us and created a bridge strong enough to
support our dreaming. Thanks for the creative courage, vision, and genius.
Also thanks to the musicians, singers, and the voice shaping the spoken
words. *Testimony* would not have been possible without you. Jackie and
Joe, though you've already crossed to the other side, thanks for giving your
voices to our words and music. Now hard work (I'm grateful to the people
at the ABC and the Sydney Opera House who embraced the project early
on) continues to nudge us along on a voyage. Thanks to the Australian Art
Orchestra for helping to keep the dream alive. Nigel, thanks for the beauty
of your stage design. Sascha, your initial praise for *Testimony* helped
me believe in this tome for Bird. Thanks go to the people at Wesleyan
University Press who take *Testimony* across a new bridge. Thanks to all of
you who love music.

—*Yusef Komunyakaa*

It has been my deep pleasure to work on this book, and I thank Wesleyan
University Press for asking me to be the project editor. I would like to
thank Yusef Komunyakaa for the invaluable contribution he has made
to the poetry world, and for his grace, patience and kindness throughout
the process of putting this book and music together. Thank you to Sandy
Evans for her cheerful and tireless help with so much for so long—from
tracking musicians, to sharing stories, to helping us find the correct infor-
mation . . . and for sharing her musical genius with the universe. I offer
deep gratitude to Christopher Williams for putting Yusef and Sandy to-
gether thereby igniting the energy that lives within these pages.

Thanks to all of the musicians for answering our emails, phone calls and
letters, and for believing we would pull this off. Thank you to Pat Sergo at

the Australian Broadcasting Corporation for granting distributor's rights for the music. To each of our brilliant contributors: Australia's fantastic jazz editor, journalist, essayist and novelist, Miriam Zolin; director/ producer, Christopher Williams; artistic director, Paul Grabowsky; and especially writer/editor/professor, Sascha Feinstein who gave us a foreword beautiful beyond words, granted us permission for reprinting his interviews and articles, and shared his advice on fine-tuning our early manuscript—thank you. Thanks too, Thierry Demont, who helped secure the Claxton family's permission to use William Claxton's incredible photo, *Charlie 'Bird' Parker, La Crescenta,* on our cover. We couldn't be more pleased. And, I offer my sincere gratitude to Wesleyan University Press director and editor-in-chief, Suzanna Tamminen, for always coming through with the hard work and humor it takes to make a book; and for entrusting me with so much of this endeavor.

This book and music package would not have survived without funding from New York University and a generous grant from the National Endowment for the Arts. Thank you.

It takes many hands to make a project like this come together. So, many thanks are also due to our cheerful student interns, the amazing Wesleyan University Press group—Leslie Starr, Parker Smathers and Stephanie Elliott—our patient spouses, our children and our friends. . . .

And of course, thank *you,* Charlie Parker.

—*Victoria Stahl, project editor*

TESTIMONY
The Recording

All music composed by Sandy Evans except where indicated.
Words by Yusef Komunyakaa

PART I

1. TESTIMONY OVERTURE *2:06*
"Moose the Mooche," Charlie Parker, Atlantic Music Corporation. "Relaxin' at Camarillo," Charlie Parker, Songs of Universal, Inc. "Dewey Square," Charlie Parker, Atlantic Music Corporation. "52nd Street Theme," Thelonious Monk, Embassy Music Corporation. Arrangement by Sandy Evans. Bernie McGann (alto saxophone); Sandy Evans (tenor saxophone); Casey Greene (baritone saxophone, flute); Paul Cutlan (bass clarinet); Warwick Alder (trumpet); Bob Coassin (trumpet); James Greening (trombone); John Rodgers (violin); Alister Spence (piano, keyboards); Lloyd Swanton (bass); Hamish Stuart (drums).

2. BOXCARS *4:06*
Michael Edward-Stevens (spoken words); Paul Cutlan (alto sax, clarinet, bass clarinet); Sandy Evans (tenor saxophone); Casey Greene (flute); Warwick Alder (trumpet); Alister Spence (keyboards); Dave Brewer (guitar); Lloyd Swanton (bass); Hamish Stuart (drums).

3. CHICKEN SHACK PART 1 *2:08*
Music: "If I Had You," Irving Berlin, Irving Berlin Music Company. Michael Edward-Stevens (spoken words); Chuck Yates (piano).

4. CHICKEN SHACK PART 2 *4:20*
Music: "Ko Ko" Charlie Parker, Atlantic Music Corporation. Michael Edward-Stevens (spoken words); Bernie McGann (alto saxophone), Warwick Alder (trumpet); Chuck Yates (piano); Jonathan Zwartz (bass); Alan Turnbull (drums).

5. PURPLE DRESS *8:44*
Kristen Cornwell (vocals); Sandy Evans (tenor saxophone); Jeremy Sawkins (guitar); Jonathan Zwartz (bass); Hamish Stuart (drums).

6. DEEP SOUTH *5:03*
Kate Swadling (vocals); Paul Cutlan (alto saxophone [alto solo], bass clarinet, clarinet); Bernie McGann (alto saxophone); Sandy Evans (tenor saxophone); Casey Greene (baritone saxophone); Bob Coassin (trumpet); James Greening (trombone); Alister Spence (trombone); Lloyd Swanton (bass); Hamish Stuart (drums).

7. A DAY LIKE TODAY *4:52*
Kurt Elling (vocals); Laurence Hobgood (piano); Jonathan Zwartz (bass); Hamish Stuart (drums).

8. ABEL AND CAIN *6:31*
Jackie Orszaczky (vocals); Tina Harrod (vocals); Dave Brewer (guitar); Jackie Orszaczky (piccolo bass); Lloyd Swanton (bass); Hamish Stuart (percussion).

9. BLACK COCKATOO *7:11*
Toni Allayialis (vocals); Paul Cutlan (alto saxophone, [alto solo]); Sandy Evans (tenor saxophone); Casey Greene (baritone saxophone, flute); Bob Coassin (trumpet); Warwick Alder (trumpet); James Greening (trombone); Alister Spence (piano); Lloyd Swanton (bass); Fabian Hevia (drums, percussion).

10. CAMARILLO PART 1 *3:45*
Michael Edward-Stevens (spoken words); Sandy
Evans (soprano saxophone); Paul Cutlan (bass
clarinet, clarinet); John Rodgers (violin); Alister
Spence (piano); Hamish Stuart (drums).

11. CAMARILLO PART 2 *3:58*
Tanya Sparke (vocals); Paul Cutlan (alto
saxophone); Sandy Evans (tenor saxophone);
Alister Spence (piano); Lloyd Swanton (bass);
Hamish Stuart (drums).

PART II

1. ADDIE'S BOY *4:46*
Pamela Knowles (vocals); Bernie McGann (alto
saxophone); Chuck Yates (piano); Jonathan
Zwartz (bass); Alan Turnbull (drums).

2. PREE'S FUNERAL SONG *6:10*
Michael Edward-Stevens (spoken words); Tina
Harrod (vocals); James Greening (trombone,
pocket trumpet); Lachlan Doley (organ);
Jonathan Zwartz (bass); Hamish Stuart (drums).

3. BARROW STREET *4:50*
Joe "Bebop" Lane (vocals); Jonathan Zwartz
(bass).

4. MOOSE THE MOOCHE *5:01*
Charlie Parker, Atlantic Music Corporation. Joe
"Bebop" Lane (vocals); Bernie McGann (alto
saxophone); Warwick Alder (trumpet); Chuck
Yates (piano); Jonathan Zwartz (bass); Alan
Turnbull (drums).

5. A SOFT TOUCH FOR STRINGS *10:38*
Michele Morgan (vocals); John Rodgers
(violin); Steve Elphick (bass); Simon Barker
(drums).

6. BARONESS PANNONICA *7:28*
Lily Dior (vocals); John Rodgers (violin);
Bernie McGann (alto saxophone); Sandy Evans
(tenor saxophone); Paul Cutlan (bass clarinet);
Warwick Alder (trumpet); James Greening
(trombone); Alister Spence (piano); Lloyd
Swanton (bass); Hamish Stuart (drums).

7. TESTIMONY FINALE *1:59*
Based on "Dewey Square," Charlie Parker,
Atlantic Music Corporation. Arrangement by
Sandy Evans. Michael Edward-Stevens (spoken
words); Sandy Evans (tenor saxophone, soprano
saxophone, flute); Warwick Alder (trumpet);
James Greening (bass trombone); Alister Spence
(piano); Jonathan Zwartz (bass); Hamish Stuart
(drums).

8. TESTIMONY CODA *1:46*
Lily Dior (vocals); Bernie McGann (alto
saxophone); Chuck Yates (piano).

(P) 2013 Australian Broadcasting Corporation

RECORDING LICENSED COURTESY OF AUSTRALIAN BROADCASTING CORPORATION

Producer: Christopher Williams
Musical Director: Sandy Evans
Music Producer: Tony Gorman
Executive Producer: Richard Buckham
Recording Engineers: Russell Stapleton and Steven Tilley; Mal Stanley—Track 6, CD 1 Mixing
Engineer: Russell Stapleton
Mastered by Russell Stapleton

Recorded 1999, Studio 227, ABC Ultimo (Sydney)
All music used by permission.